STRONG
IN THE *Wounded Heart...*
LIVING IN THE LIGHT!

I0555362

Dr. RoseMary Cairo, EdD, LCPC
Alberto Minzer, M. Div, LCSW, CADC

Strong in the Wounded Heart....Living in the Light was not written to impose the religious or spiritual values of the authors. It is up to the reader to find one's strength and light in God, the ultimate universal energy, and to build a relationship with God through one's chosen faith or spiritual practice.

It is our suggestion that the reader fills out the spiritual assessment on page 139

Dr. RoseMary Cairo:

I dedicate this book to the 3 greatest gifts in my life, my children, Daniella, Krystal & Drew and my beloved grandchildren, Hunter, Brayden, Everley, Mason, Lyla, Stella, Sophia & Johnny. Together they have been my greatest teachers of what love is and the importance of living in the light of God.

Alberto Minzer:

To all those that have brought me to the darkest places, thank you for helping me to embrace the light. To my children, Kara & Rachel, my grandchildren Joseph, Isaac, and Iryeh and my wife Phyllis who brings light into my life.

Acknowledgements

Dr. RoseMary Cairo:

Jesus put me on this spiritual path of enlightenment at an early age to condition me to be an emissary in a world of light and darkness and to share my testimony of faith and miracles. It is through Him that I found the words to write.

Through life's experiences, the love, joy and challenges, I am grateful. For each person that has grown my heart and those that have scarred it, you have each taught me the lessons needed to be learned. My sincere appreciation to all that was, is and will be while on this life journey, as I continue to grow in faith, love and purpose!

Alberto Minzer:

Without Gods inspiration this book would not have been published. His light has been the source of my life. I also like to acknowledge all of my patients who have taught me about the wounded heart and shown me the resilience of the human spirit.

I would like to thank the following individuals.

Dr. Ibrahim Jaffe, Dr. Kamila Carolyn Shenmen, Jannah Bianca Guerra, MDiv, BSPT, PT, ICC, CMH, Dr. Judith Sharifa Keith, Dr. Maxine Salima Adelstein, Mahabbah Young, Anton Nasir Possenig, Latif Sorensen MDvi and Sara Madonna.

A special thanks to Huda Khadijah for her steadfast, boundless faith in me, her loving championing of my path, I will always carry you in my heart.

This book is a loving collaboration of two individuals who have done a great deal of soul-searching and want to share the gift of light to others who are seeking to further connect with God's light. As you proceed to read this book, allow yourself to open your heart and embrace the light of God...

Contents

Prologue

This book intends to wake you up and help you make conscious decisions about how to live your life and be accountable to your heart! This book is written to give you added knowledge, confirm that which you may already know, and understand your vital part in the evolution of your soul. The world is changing exponentially, and it is imperative to embrace the light and not fall into the darkness. Humanity is being squeezed by God, challenging us to choose Him, the light where truth prevails and is void of lies and false promises.

The fact that you are reading this book means that you want to understand how to heal your heart, to be a light-keeper, and part of the life force. It begins by healing your heart, which then emanates to those around you and the healing of others begins. Don't let the world distract you with meaningless noise, as it seduces you through false promises, social media and attachments. Don't allow others to pull you away from living in God's light. The darkness of the world is intentionally trying to kidnap you away from your source, alluring you and tempting you with false beliefs. Instead, be an emissary of light by first living in the light and then committing to serve and help others to get there. This is how a positive transformation in the world begins. We are all responsible!

Chapter 1
The Wounded Heart

A wounded heart does not heal by forgetting, it heals by being gently seen, held, and loved back to life.

– Alberto Minzer

We use the term wounded heart often, but what does it truly mean? When you cut your arm, you can see the wound. It bleeds, infects, scabs and scars. The healing is complete. What happens with a wounded heart? Emotional wounds can't be seen. The cut can be deep, and it bleeds, but if not cared for, emotions fester as the wound is ignored. Like an infection, it becomes toxic and impacts your emotions. Eventually, heart wounds are scabbed over, but when *triggered* by a similar emotional experience, the scab gets picked off and it bleeds again. This is an automatic response of an unhealed wound, one that hasn't scarred because the healing is incomplete. These wounds can take a lifetime to heal unless you lean into the pain, understand the reason for the experience, release the pain to God and turn to His light, the light of God, of authentic love and ultimate truth. The longer we ignore the wound, the greater the long-term impact influences our lives. The phrase "a hole in the soul" is a metaphor for a deep wound that hasn't been healed through the above process. It's a disconnect from the deliberate intention of healing through the light and love of God. This hole can be recognized as negative emotions, health issues, dysregulation, addictions, discontent, victimization, obsessive-compulsive behavior, anxiety, depression, the state of continued anger, eating disorders, workaholism, dysfunctional behaviors and more. Does this speak to you? Have you assessed your religious and/or spiritual practice?

Through the practice of breathing techniques, meditation, mindfulness, and prayer, you may find the answers that can lead you to the light. If you want change, healing, and recovery, you won't find it in life's distractions. This is darkness that wants to pull you away from the light. You must turn off the noise of the outside world and look within where the deepest truth resides. Here, you will find the stillness necessary to assess your spiritual connection, where healing and inner growth occur.

The Nature of Wounds

A wounded heart is something we all experience at some point. Whether through loss, betrayal, disappointment, or trauma, these wounds can feel overwhelming, as if they have the power to break us. In our wounded state, we may question our worth, our purpose, and even God's presence in our lives. Yet, it is precisely within this brokenness that God's light shines the brightest.

Our wounds are not signs of weakness. Instead, they are part of what makes us human. They are evidence of a life fully lived, where love has been given and risks have been taken. When we carry these wounds, they become an invitation to rely on something greater than ourselves. The light of God enters through these cracks in our heart, offering healing and transforming our pain into strength.

How We Begin to Heal the Wounded Heart

Healing begins by having the physical and emotional awareness that there's a disconnect. Often one turns away from the memory of the experience, putting it on the shelf or repressing it deep in one's heart. You can feel this emotion as it constricts your heart. This is a symptom given by God as a trigger for you to do the work. This is when it is time to face the emotional pain that is trapped in your heart. If not, it bleeds into interpersonal relationships, impacting our ability to commune happily with others, to feel inner peace and fulfillment in life.

Acknowledging the Pain

The first step in healing the wounded heart is to acknowledge the pain that exists. Many people try to ignore or suppress their emotional hurt, hoping that time alone will make it disappear. However, healing cannot begin until we face the reality of what has wounded us. It requires courage to admit that we are hurting, and it may even require confronting deep-seated fear, shame, or unresolved grief. By acknowledging the pain, we open the door to healing. It's important to allow yourself to feel the full range of emotions, including sadness, anger, confusion, or even numbness. These emotions are valid responses to the wounds of the heart and should not be rushed through or dismissed.

Allowing Yourself to Grieve

Grief is a natural part of healing. When we experience loss, whether it's the death of a loved one, the end of a relationship, or the loss of a dream, it can leave a void in our hearts. Grieving is the process of coming to terms with that void, allowing us to express and process the deep sorrow and longing that accompany the wound.

The grieving process can take time and looks different for everyone. Some people need to talk about their feelings, while others may need solitude and reflection. There's no right or wrong way to grieve. What's important is to honor your feelings, give yourself permission to mourn, and trust that, in time, the weight of grief will lighten.

Seeking Support and Connection

Healing the wounded heart is not something that needs to be done alone. In fact, one of the most powerful ways to heal is by seeking support from others. Friends, family, mentors, religious figures, and counselors can offer a safe space to share your emotions, provide comfort and remind you that you're not alone in your pain.

Connection with others allows you to feel seen, heard, and validated. It helps to break the isolation that often comes with emotional wounds. If the pain is too deep to handle on your own, seeking professional help from a therapist can be a significant step. Therapy provides tools for navigating difficult emotions, understanding the roots of the wound, and finding ways to move forward.

The Transformation of the Wounded Heart

Living in your heart is not a destination but an ongoing journey. It is about embracing each moment with love, compassion, and authenticity. This path invites us to look inward, quiet the noise of the outside world, and trust the wisdom that arises from within. By cultivating a heart-centered way of being, we connect more deeply with ourselves and with others, creating a ripple effect of kindness and understanding. The heart becomes a guide, leading us to live a life of purpose, peace, and genuine fulfillment. This is where true happiness resides, deep within the heart, always available if we choose to take accountability.

The journey of healing a wounded heart is a deeply personal and transformative process. Life inevitably brings moments of pain, loss, and betrayal, leaving emotional scars that can feel overwhelming. Whether the wound comes from broken relationships, grief, trauma, or disappointment, the healing of the heart is essential for finding peace, wholeness, and the capacity to love again.

Chapter 2
The Power of Spiritual Surrender

A sacrifice to be real must cost, must hurt, and must empty ourselves. Give yourself fully to God. He will use you to accomplish great things on the condition that you believe much more in His love than in your weakness.

-*Mother Teresa*

The key to self-healing is often found in spiritual surrender. While healing can involve many aspects, such as physical, emotional, and psychological transformation, it frequently comes through letting go of the need to control and instead trusting in a higher power beyond oneself. Stating that I am in control of my life is the paradox that one needs to understand. God is at the helm of life, and we are given every opportunity to understand this. If we don't, we are misguided and can open doors that lead to darkness, never being fully satisfied because there is an emptiness in your soul that belongs only to God and only He can fill it. Not surrendering to Him will keep you chasing happiness that can't be received. If you don't choose God, He will come to you with more challenging experiences so you can have the opportunity to lean on him and ask Him for help.

Spiritual surrender does not mean giving up or resigning to a fate of suffering. Rather, it is the act of releasing attachment to outcomes, expectations, and the need to control every aspect of life. It involves acknowledging our limitations as human beings and opening our hearts and minds to divine guidance, grace, and wisdom. When we surrender, we are no longer trying to force solutions or resist what is; we allow healing to unfold naturally, trusting that divine intelligence is at work.

In the context of self-healing, spiritual surrender can look like relinquishing the need to have all the answers, accepting that some pain or circumstances are beyond our immediate understanding, and having faith that in time, healing will come. This process allows for peace to replace the anxiety that often accompanies the struggle for control and the fear of the unknown.

One of the biggest obstacles to healing is our attachment to how we think things should be. We often carry expectations about how life, health, or relationships should unfold. Unrealized expectations can lead to frustration, disappointment, and prolonged emotional suffering. Spiritual surrender invites us to release those expectations and embrace the present moment as it is.

This doesn't mean passivity or inaction, it means doing what we can to care for ourselves and others while trusting that God is handling the larger picture. When we let go of our need to control, we stop fighting against reality and allow room for growth, learning, and healing.

At the core of spiritual surrender is trusting in something greater than us. For most, this is faith in God; for others, it could be a sense of connection to the universe. Trusting in a benevolent force and process allows us to relax into the present and open ourselves to possibilities we might not have imagined.

Trust is powerful because it helps us navigate through uncertainty, fear, and pain. In times of difficulty, trusting in something larger than our individual selves offers comfort and a sense of safety. It helps us believe that healing, though sometimes slow or painful, is possible.

• Key principle: "Trust in the Lord with all your heart and lean not on your own understanding." (Proverbs 3:5)

This passage reminds us that while we may not always understand the reasons behind our suffering, spiritual surrender allows us to find peace in the unknown, confident that healing is unfolding in ways we may not immediately see.

Acceptance is a key part of spiritual surrender. Often, our resistance to pain, loss, or hardship exacerbates our suffering. By accepting our current situation, whether it be illness, emotional hurt, or trauma, we need to stop fighting against reality and make space for healing.

Acceptance does not mean condoning harmful behaviors or situations. Rather, it means recognizing what is happening in the present moment without trying to deny, resist, or escape it. Acceptance is about facing reality with grace and surrendering the need to have everything go our way. Once we accept what is, we can begin to work toward change or healing from a place of peace rather than resistance, which is a negative energy.

Allowing Divine Grace to Flow

When we surrender spiritually, we open ourselves to the flow of divine grace. Grace is unmerited favor from God. It acts as divine assistance, enabling individuals to overcome challenges and achieve spiritual goals. It is the unearned, loving presence of God that supports us in our healing journey. It is the force that fills the gaps where we fall short, and it carries us through our darkest moments.

By surrendering, we acknowledge that we do not have to heal or navigate life's challenges alone. There is something greater guiding and holding us through the process.

Divine grace often shows up in unexpected ways, through the kindness of others, through sudden insights, and through moments of peace that wash over us during difficult times. By surrendering, we can receive God's grace to work within us, healing not just the surface wounds but the deep spiritual and emotional layers that need attention.

Spiritual surrender also involves patience. Healing, whether physical, emotional, or spiritual, often takes time. Our culture is often focused on quick fixes and instant results, but deep healing requires patience and a willingness to remain present with the process.

Surrender means allowing healing to take the time it needs. It means staying present in the moment, even when that moment is uncomfortable or painful. By cultivating patience, we give space for the healing process to unfold in its own time. We stop rushing toward the end goal and start finding peace in each step along the way.

Moving from Fear to Love

A crucial aspect of spiritual surrender is the shift from fear to love. When we try to control life, we are often operating from a place of fear, fear of the unknown, fear of pain, fear of vulnerability.

Surrendering spiritually invites us to let go of that fear and instead place our trust in love, love for ourselves, love for others, and love for the Divine.

This shift allows us to approach healing, not with anxiety or desperation but with compassion and trust. It helps us recognize that even in our woundedness, we are worthy of love and care. In moments of spiritual surrender, we let go of fear's grip and open ourselves to the transformative power of love, which is essential for true healing.

Spiritual surrender is a powerful key to self-healing. It teaches us to let go of control, to trust in the Divine, and to find peace in the midst of uncertainty. By releasing expectations, embracing patience, and allowing grace to work within us, we create the space needed for deep healing to occur. Surrendering spiritually does not mean passivity; rather, it means actively choosing to trust in the process of healing, to accept what is, and to move forward with faith, knowing that we are being guided and supported every step of the way. Through surrender, we learn that healing is not something we achieve on our own, it is a collaborative process with the Divine, one that transforms not only our heart wounds but also our entire way of being.

Healing the heart is also about reconnecting with yourself. When we are wounded, we often lose touch with our sense of self-worth, our inner joy, and our purpose. Part of healing involves nurturing your spirit and rediscovering what makes you feel alive, loved, and whole.

This might mean engaging in self-care practices, exploring creative outlets, or spending time in nature. It may also involve reflecting on your values, setting boundaries, or practicing prayer, mindfulness and meditations. Reconnecting with yourself means treating your heart with the same compassion and care you would offer to someone else in pain.

For many, faith and spirituality are powerful sources of comfort and healing. Belief in God and committing to spiritual practices, can provide a sense of hope, purpose, and strength amid emotional pain. Trusting that there is meaning beyond the hurt, that healing is possible, and that you are being guided through the process can help ease the burden of carrying a wounded heart.

Spiritual practices such as prayer, meditation, or reading sacred texts can bring peace and perspective. Many find that in surrendering their pain to a higher power, they are able to release control and find solace in the belief that healing will come in due time.

While no one wishes for emotional pain, wounds can be a source of growth and transformation. Healing a wounded heart often leads to greater self-awareness, resilience, and empathy for others. The process teaches you about your own strength, your capacity to endure, and your ability to find beauty in brokenness.

Many who have healed from deep emotional wounds go on to help others, offering their wisdom and compassion to those who are suffering. In this way, the wound becomes not just a source of pain but a path to a greater purpose and connection with the world.

Healing the wounded heart is a journey that requires time, patience, and care. It is not a linear process, and there will be moments of progress, as well as setbacks. However, with each step toward healing, through grieving, forgiveness, seeking support, and spiritual connection, the heart begins to mend. Over time, the pain softens, and in its place grows a deeper understanding of yourself, a renewed sense of hope, and the capacity to love again.

Though the scars may remain, they can serve as reminders of your resilience and your journey toward wholeness. Healing is possible, and with it comes the opportunity to embrace life fully once again, with a heart that has learned *to find strength even in its wounded places.*

Becoming aware of the nature and symptoms of the emotional experience, how it has impacted you physically and emotionally, as well as in your relationships with others and God, are the first steps toward healing the wounded heart. It is necessary to acknowledge the feeling of brokenness and the need to heal. The next step is to better understand the lesson

14

within the experience, what it has taught you and why. Remember that on a spiritual level you allowed the experience. All lessons come from God to help you grow and become closer to Him. This can be very challenging, but it is necessary to be accountable. Without this step, there is no forgiveness of self, others, or God, and without forgiveness, you can't live in the light. Through the process of beginning with awareness and ending with forgiveness, we heal the wounded heart. It is then that we have the opportunity to connect with the light, the love of God, where the purification occurs to heal the wounded heart and learn the lesson necessary to evolve spiritually, love authentically and know inner peace and harmony.

Chapter 3
Living in the Light

People are like stained glass windows. They sparkle and shine when the sun is out, but when the darkness sets in, their true beauty is revealed only if there is a light from within

-Elisabeth Kubler-Ross

What is the LIGHT? There are no words worthy to describe *The Light*. It is ethereal and divine. It is of the celestial world, it is the essence of God, and *His* love that fills our spirit. It connects us to our higher self. For the non-believers, this light is concealed. It takes faith to open the portal to this light. A good person who is a non-believer that doesn't believe in God doesn't have the key to open the portal. The key is faith, the certainty in the existence of God.

Love is limited to non-believers because authentic agape love comes from the light of God. Living in the light begins with feeling God's love. At birth, a baby is filled with spiritual light. The light of God is gifted at the creation of each soul. At the onset of life, we all know His pure love. Through life experiences, culture, and the influence of caregivers, children can begin to separate themselves from this love. They can continue to grow without the deliberate intention of being connected to God. Here is where the light can begin to dissipate. As children experiences trauma and/or

emotional pain, they can begin to drift from the Creator. The heart wounds can begin to separate the child from God and the light becomes dim if not encouraged by caregivers. How do children fill this separation, this gap that begins to grow into adulthood, if not attended to? How are children reminded that the ultimate love, peace, and hopefulness come from their relationship with the Lord? It is the Emissaries of Light, the adult believers, those that are on the spiritual path with God that are responsible for sharing their faith and their testimonies and to feed these children the living water that created their souls. The ultimate feeling they thirst for is the agape love they received from God in their creation. If lost, there becomes a continued search, often becoming a quest throughout life where self-medicating becomes a delusional substitute for this ultimate love. We were designed to choose God. It doesn't happen without choice. Choice is the fundamental ingredient to connect with God's light.

Fear is the Opposite of Love

On Earth, there are two energies that are the root of all emotions; fear, which comes from the ego and love, which comes from God. Which do you choose? Living a human experience feeds our ego with the desire for greed and self-pleasure, and its mission is to tear us away and separate us from God's light. The human need for power and control is a human condition with false beliefs. God is the ultimate power, and control is an illusion. Surrendering to God is acknowledging that we are servants to Him and to realize the true nature of our existence. All actions are a choice. One must learn to align with the light to feel ultimate peace and be healed. Being intentional is imperative. Prayer, through dialogue with God, chanting His name and singing His praise are ways to feel God's light working within you. It is only through the light of God and the essence of His love that our heart can know divine love and heal from life's challenging experiences. The ethereal heart that embodies our emotions is the center of our being. It is infinite and the home of our soul. Knowing God's light is delivered through intention. This intention is the deliberate choice to be aligned with God and is the way to know Him and feel His love again.

The separation from the light of God is where darkness lives and evil thrives. There is no grace or mercy in the absence of God's love. The doors of Satan open with false promises and with the 7 sins: Pride, Envy, Gluttony, Lust, Anger, Greed and Sloth.

The remedy to defeat Satan exists in the heart and surrendering to God. We must lock every door and purify these sins, cutting the roots of evil. Being conscious of the power of God and His love for you is the answer. We must be deliberate in thought and action. Here is where the purity of the heart can be created. God is the Almighty and can banish all evil. Know His power and be sincere in your cry for His forgiveness and feel His love. This is a choice!

It is through the light of God that a broken heart begins to heal. It is in the emotional pain that we can develop growth edges, where pruning occurs, and we can ultimately blossom in His light. There is one tree that stands for love, peace, and harmony, but many branches exist that give us optional ways to live in love and God's light.

Living in God's light involves aligning your life with His teachings, seeking His presence, and letting His love guide your actions. Here are some ways to live in God's light:

1. *Seek God Through Prayer*

Spend time talking to God daily. Prayer builds a personal relationship with Him, allowing His light to guide you in every area of life.

2. *Study His Word*

Read and meditate on Scripture to understand His will and promises. The Bible serves as a lamp to your feet and a light to your path (Psalm 119:105).

3. *Live With Love and Kindness*

Reflect God's love by showing compassion, forgiveness, and care for others. Jesus teaches us to love one another as He has loved us (John 13:34).

4. *Walk in Obedience*

Follow God's commandments and live a life that honors Him. Obedience to His Word allows His light to shine through your actions.

5. *Surround Yourself with Godly Community*

Fellowship with others who are also seeking to walk in God's light. Together, you can encourage, pray, and grow in faith.

6. *Confess and Turn from Sin*

Be honest with God about your struggles, repent, and ask for His forgiveness. Sin dims God's light in your life. Living in the light means embracing a life rooted in truth, love, and righteousness, guided by God's presence. It involves walking away from darkness, sin, fear, and doubt and choosing to reflect God's goodness in your daily actions.

Chapter 4
Grief

Grief is love with nowhere to go; Healing begins when we learn to carry that love forward.

-Alberto Minzer

Grief is a natural part of healing. When we experience loss, it leaves a void in our hearts. Grieving is the process of coming to terms with that void, allowing us to express and process the deep sorrow and longing that accompany this wound.

The grieving process can take time and looks different for everyone. Some people need to talk about their feelings, while others may need solitude and reflection. There's no right or wrong way to grieve. What's important is to honor your feelings, permit yourself to mourn, and trust that, in time, the weight of grief will lighten.

The Journey of Healing Grief

Grief is a profound, universal experience that comes to each of us at some point in life. It might follow the loss of a loved one, the end of a relationship, the passing of a cherished pet, or the disappearance of a dream we once held close. In its wake, grief can be isolating, overwhelming, and relentless. Yet, while it often feels like a deep wound that will never fully heal, with time, compassion, and support, healing becomes possible.

Understanding Grief as a Journey

Grief is not something that can be rushed or skipped. It is a journey unique to each individual, with no universal timeline. There may be days when you feel almost normal and others when the pain feels as raw as if it had just happened. It's important to acknowledge that grief is not linear. It can come in waves, bringing unexpected moments of sadness, anger, relief, guilt, or even joy as memories surface.

Some frameworks, like the *Five Stages of Grief* by Elisabeth Kübler-Ross, describe common stages: denial, anger, bargaining, depression, and acceptance. But grief is often more fluid, with emotions intertwining and resurfacing. Recognizing that this fluctuation is natural can bring some comfort. Rather than viewing grief as a series of milestones, think of it as a landscape to be navigated, one step at a time.

The First Steps:

Allowing Yourself to Grieve

Healing begins with permission to feel whatever arises. In a culture that often encourages us to be "strong" and "move on," grief can feel like an inconvenience or even a weakness. But the reality is that acknowledging and honoring your pain is a vital part of healing. Allow yourself to cry, to be angry, to feel lost. Suppressing grief only prolongs its grip on our hearts and minds, while allowing it to flow creates space for healing.

If you find it difficult to express your grief, try journaling, painting, or another creative outlet. These can become safe spaces to release emotions, providing relief without needing words. Remember, there's no need to explain or justify your grief. Every loss, no matter how small or large, deserves compassion and attention.

Seeking Support and Finding Connection

Grief can feel like a profoundly isolating experience, yet connection with others often becomes the lifeline that pulls us back from despair. Speaking with family members or friends, attending support groups, or seeking counseling can offer relief. Sharing your story with others allows you to realize that you're not alone and that many have walked a similar path. When those around you are unable to understand the depth of your feelings, connecting with a therapist trained in grief counseling can be an invaluable support.

Support groups for people who have lost loved ones can offer a sense of solidarity. Sometimes, simply knowing others are there, even in silence, brings comfort. Lean into the connections that bring you peace and give yourself permission to take a step back from those that bring additional strain.

Honoring and Remembering a Loved One

Healing is not about forgetting; it's about learning to live with the memory of what or whom you have lost. Finding ways to honor your loved one can create a healthy relationship with the past, allowing you to carry the essence of what you've lost forward with you. This can be as simple as lighting a candle, creating a memory book, visiting a place of shared meaning, or establishing a ritual that keeps the memory alive in a loving way.

If you are healing from the loss of a relationship or a past dream, honoring that chapter of your life can be a powerful way to find closure. Write a letter to yourself or to the other person (even if you don't send it), thanking them or acknowledging the ways they shaped your life. Recognizing that this person mattered helps with letting go, not of the memories, but of the pain.

Rebuilding a New Normal

Eventually, you may start to feel the desire to rebuild. This is a time of tentative steps, learning to envision a future without the presence of what you've lost. As you rebuild, consider creating a new "normal" that honors your grief rather than erasing it. It's okay if things don't go back to exactly how they were; sometimes, healing creates a new version of ourselves that reflects the love and loss we've experienced.

Begin this journey with small steps that feel manageable. Reclaim interests that may have been set aside, try new activities, and open yourself to connections. As you begin to engage in life again, there may be moments of guilt or sadness. These feelings are natural. You are not "moving on" in a way that dismisses what you've lost. Rather, you are learning to live alongside it, allowing yourself to grow around the loss.

Practicing Self-Compassion and Mindfulness

Grief often brings complicated feelings, like guilt, regret, or even relief, especially if the loss follows a period of prolonged suffering. It's essential to approach these feelings with compassion. Be gentle with yourself. Practice mindfulness to help you stay present with whatever you are feeling in the moment, without judgment. Meditation, breathing exercises, and quiet reflection can help ground you when grief feels overwhelming.

Try to practice small acts of self-care each day, even if they feel forced or pointless at first. Take a walk, prepare a nourishing meal or rest. These small moments of care remind you that, even in the heartbreak and pain, you are worthy of love and kindness.

Finding Meaning and Growth in Grief

In time, some people find that grief changes them in profound ways, sparking personal growth, deepening empathy, or reshaping values and priorities. This doesn't mean that the pain was "worth it" or that it's fair to endure such loss. Rather, it's an acknowledgment that even in hardship, we can find purpose and resilience. If it feels right, consider ways to channel your grief into something meaningful, such as volunteer work, creative expression, helping others who are grieving, or simply living with greater awareness of life's fragility and beauty.

Embracing the Unpredictable Path of Healing

Grief never completely disappears. Even as you heal, there will be days when the sadness returns. Reminders will come unexpectedly, a song, a scent, a memory. Allow these moments to come and go without judging your progress. Each of these moments can be seen as part of the journey, signs that what or who you loved has left a permanent mark on your heart. And, in that sense, they remind us of the gift of having loved deeply.

As you continue on this journey, know that you are not alone. Healing from grief is possible, even if it feels out of reach now. One step at a time, you will learn to carry the weight of your loss with strength, honoring the past while embracing the future that awaits. In time, when living in God's light, the landscape of grief, once dark and unfamiliar, will become part of your story, a testament to both the sorrow and the resilience of the human spirit.

Many people find that faith in God can be a powerful source of comfort, strength, and healing during the grief process. Spiritual beliefs can offer a framework for understanding loss and provide practices, teachings, and a sense of connection that helps navigate grief's complex emotions.

While the way God helps with grief is unique to each person's beliefs and experiences, here are some common ways in which faith can be a source of solace and support:

1. <u>A Source of Comfort and Peace</u>

In times of grief, many turn to prayer, scripture, or meditation to feel God's presence and find comfort. Prayer or meditation allows for a quiet space where one can express feelings, ask for help, or simply feel God's love and peace. Passages like Psalm 34:18, "The Lord is close to the brokenhearted and saves those who are crushed in spirit", offer reassurance that God is near in times of deep sorrow. Even in moments of despair, the belief in God's unwavering presence can bring peace and consolation.

2. <u>A Sense of Purpose and Hope</u>

For those who believe in an afterlife or a divine plan, faith can give grief a sense of purpose or meaning. The idea that a loved one has gone to a peaceful, eternal place can be incredibly comforting, or if a dream to be fulfilled doesn't seem possible, it can be because God is protecting you. Many people find solace in the belief that God has a plan that, even if it isn't fully understood now, holds greater wisdom. This perspective can help ease feelings of despair and hopelessness by focusing on the idea that, in time, there will be reunions, healing, or deeper understanding.

3. <u>Strength and Resilience</u>

Faith in God can give people the strength to face each day. Even when the pain seems too heavy to bear, many find that turning to God helps them to feel grounded and fortified. Scriptures, teachings, or hymns that emphasize God's strength and guidance remind believers that they don't have to face grief alone. This trust can bring an inner strength to take each step forward, even on the hardest days.

4. <u>A Community of Support</u>

Faith often connects people to a community of others who can provide love, compassion, and support. Church groups, prayer groups, or spiritual friends often provide a network that can listen, offer prayers, and share words of comfort. In times of loss, feeling part of a community that can physically and emotionally support the bereaved can be invaluable. Sharing grief within a faith-based community reminds people that they are not alone in their journey and that they are surrounded by others who can carry them when the weight feels too heavy.

5. <u>A Means to Express Grief</u>

Religious practices and rituals provide a way to express grief in a sacred context, which can be profoundly healing. Many faiths offer formal or informal rituals for mourning, such as lighting candles, saying specific prayers, or holding memorial services for those who have passed. These practices not only honor the deceased but allow the grieving to feel close to God and their faith. Engaging in these rituals can provide structure in a time when everything feels uncertain and can give people a way to process their emotions with reverence and intentionality.

6. <u>Learning to Surrender and Trust</u>

Grief often brings complex feelings of anger, regret, guilt, or even questioning of one's faith. This is natural, and faith in God can actually encourage the grieving to bring all emotions, even difficult ones, into their spiritual life. Trusting that God can hold the fullness of one's grief, including anger and confusion, can be a relief. Many find that surrendering their pain to God, rather than bearing it alone, helps them feel lighter and supported. Faith can encourage letting go, accepting the mystery of life and death, and trusting that God is guiding them through the unknown.

7. <u>Growth, Healing, and Transformation</u>

Many believe that God can use grief as a means of spiritual growth and transformation. While this doesn't mean that grieving is any less painful, it reflects the idea that grief, with time and faith, can deepen compassion, empathy, and love for others. Through the process, some discover a renewed appreciation for life, a closer relationship with God, and a greater capacity to help others who are grieving. This spiritual growth doesn't erase the loss but transforms it into a path toward healing, meaning, and deeper faith.

8. <u>A Reminder of Divine Love</u>

In moments when the grief feels overwhelming, the assurance of God's unconditional love can be deeply comforting. Knowing that one is loved unconditionally by God, even in times of sadness, disappointment and doubt, can help people feel secure and cherished. Some people find that envisioning God's love surrounding them using meditation, visualization, and prayer gives them peace and security, a reminder that they are never truly alone in their pain.

9. <u>An Invitation to Remember and Cherish</u>

For many, faith in God encourages them to celebrate and cherish the lives of those they have lost and the dreams they have left behind. In faith, remembering is not just about sorrow but about cherishing the gift that each life brings, seeing it as part of a beautiful, eternal journey. This can transform grief from sorrow into a blend of gratitude and remembrance and to better understand that God has a plan and to trust His journey.

In summary, faith in God doesn't eliminate grief but offers a guiding light through its darkness. By finding comfort, strength, purpose, and love in God, many people discover a way to navigate their grief with resilience and hope. Whether through prayer, community, rituals, or simply trusting in a divine plan, faith can be a source of profound healing, allowing the bereaved to honor their loss while holding onto a sense of peace and purpose.

Occasionally, weep deeply over the life you hoped would be. Grieve the losses. Then wash your face. Trust God. And embrace the life you have.

- John Piper

Chapter 5
Miracles are Real

There are only two ways to live your life. One is as though nothing is a miracle. The other is as though everything is.

– Albert Einstein

Miracles are defined as a phenomenon that can't be explained by science. They are understood as an extraordinary event that goes beyond the ordinary laws of nature and are often attributed to a divine cause. People have shared their miracles for centuries. Do you believe in miracles, or do you think the unexplainable are coincidences or accidents? Believing that miracles DON'T exist is often pure ego. The ego resists what it cannot control, but the heart remains open to the possibility of the unseen.

The power of miracles lies in their ability to transcend the ordinary and awaken a deep sense of wonder, hope, and faith. Miracles often defy natural explanation, making them moments that inspire awe and lead us to consider realities beyond what we can see and understand. They are extraordinary events that remind us of the divine, the mysterious, and the possibility of transformation when we least expect it.

Miracles as Signs of the Divine

In many religious traditions, miracles are seen as direct interventions by God or a higher power, signaling divine presence in our world. They reveal the power of the supernatural in ways that human reason cannot fully grasp, acting as signs that something larger is at work in the universe. A miracle is an event in which God intervenes in the natural order for a purpose, often to reveal power, confirm faith, or bring about healing or deliverance. These events often come during times of need or crisis, offering not only physical healing or change, but also a profound spiritual message: that the divine is present and responsive to human suffering.

These miracles are the moments that point to a deeper reality: that God is active, loving, and capable of bringing restoration and renewal.

Miracles as Catalysts for Faith

Miracles have the unique power to strengthen and deepen faith. For those who experience or witness them, miracles often become pivotal moments that affirm their belief in a higher power and give them confidence in the presence of divine grace. Even for those who only hear about miracles, these stories can stir a longing for the transcendent and ignite a belief that there is more to life than the tangible and the explainable.

Miracles serve as a reminder that in a world often dominated by logic and reason, there is still room for mystery, for the unknown, and for the possibility that not everything can be controlled or predicted. They invite us to trust, even when the future seems uncertain, and to believe in the possibility of the impossible.

Miracles and Hope

One of the most profound aspects of miracles is the hope they offer. In moments of despair, when all options seem exhausted, miracles remind us that change is possible, even in the bleakest circumstances. Whether it's the unexpected recovery from an illness, a sudden provision of resources in a time of need, a long-awaited pregnancy, or an emotional breakthrough after years of struggle, miracles can bring hope when everything else feels lost.

This hope is not just about wishful thinking or longing for magic; it's rooted in the belief that the universe, the power of God, is working in ways we cannot fully understand. It reminds us that life can surprise us with goodness when we least expect it and that we are not alone in our struggles.

The Everyday Miracles

While grand and dramatic miracles are often the ones that capture our attention, there is also profound power in the smaller, quieter miracles that happen every day. The birth of a child, the healing of a broken relationship, or the kindness of a stranger can all be seen as miraculous moments reflecting life's beauty and mystery. These everyday miracles may not defy the laws of nature, but they remind us that grace, love, and transformation are constantly at work in our world.

In recognizing these smaller miracles, we cultivate a spirit of gratitude and awareness, seeing the Divine in the ordinary. We learn to appreciate the subtle ways that miracles touch our lives, often in ways that are not immediately obvious. The power of miracles lies in their ability to shift our perspective, draw us closer to the Divine, and remind us of the boundless possibilities in life. They disrupt the ordinary, offering moments of transformation that reveal the presence of something greater than us. Whether grand or small, miracles invite us to live with a sense of awe, to nurture faith, and to hold onto hope, knowing that even in the darkest times, the impossible can happen.

Chapter 6
Free Will

The question is not whether we will die but how we will live.

– Joan Borysenko

In our limited human intelligence, we don't have the comprehension of God's motivations when creating free will. We can assume that God gave us the ability to have personal choice, as it relates to our own personal spiritual development. Individually, we decide how we will conduct ourselves in our lifetime. Even though God knows our decisions, he gives us free will to determine how we will travel up the mountain of life. We will all travel the mountain, no matter race, creed, or gender, but will it be the easy path, the adventurous journey, or one of risk and danger? Those who sleep and those who live in spiritual darkness are unaware of their necessary connection to The Source, God in all His love and glory. They live in their shadow, still given opportunities to find their spiritual connection, but many are blind and ignore the opportunity for spiritual oneness with Him. Here, darkness seeps in and the separation from the light becomes reality. One of God's greatest gifts given to us is free will. The development of our soul is rooted in the choices we make. Every choice is measured by the universal laws and the ten commandments created by God for all His creation and is judged, no matter how big or small, by God's intention for us to live in the purest light. Being aligned with God's intention for us is how we live in the light. Free will allows you to co-create your life with Him. He has given us freedom of will but guides us with wisdom, discernment and intuition.

For us to gain control of our spiritual growth one must become aware and live with spiritual intention. It is waking up into a spiritual life vs. sleeping. We gain a deeper awareness of the choices we are given and the importance of acknowledging the power of each choice when living in a positive relationship with God and the deep understanding that God is ultimately in control of our lives. To live in the light, one must make the choice to surrender to God's will, and to surrender your life to glorify and serve God in the service of others, not self. Those who lay sleeping live in a physical world of ego, materialism, and the delusion of self-power through money, possessions, and self-glory. This is separation from living in the light of God. The lack of attachment to the Source brings discontent and loneliness. We are designed to be one with God. When we are separated from Him, there often develops what we call a "hole in the soul", where addiction, depression, and fear gain control. The desire to self-medicate becomes a form of addiction as it temporarily fills the soul but seeps out of the hole, creating the same feeling of emptiness and the need to refill. This behavior becomes a pattern and emptiness has no end. The heart hungers for its true connection; without it, the sleepers continue searching for wholeness, but it is impossible if not connected to God. It is only in Him that wholeness exists. Self-medicating with drugs, food, materialism, etc., can never heal the hole in the soul because it is not the connection the spirit comes here for when incarnating into this lifetime. One must be connected to God to live in joy, peace and fulfillment.

Selecting this book to read is an indication of your hunger to be living in the light and recalibrating your spiritual journey. Many are riddled with internal pain and angst and don't know why. Embracing your spiritual journey helps you to know that all experiences teach us and give us messages to learn as we travel up the mountain. Being on the journey of enlightenment gives us peace even when we are challenged and looking for the answer to the riddles we are experiencing. But when in the light, we know God is our Creator and has been intentional in our lives. It is up to us to reflect and find the answers. It's all before us; we just need to lift the fog, walk into the light and see the answers needed to move forward in our spiritual growth.

Ultimately, with God given free will, we have the choice to be actively aware of how we want to live. We choose to believe or not to believe, and it is a choice to live in the light and have inner joy and ultimate peace within us. It's important to understand that we are a spindle in God's wheel. It is He who holds our life force and the gavel to assess who we are and how we have lived our lives. Life and eternity are determined by choices. This is the time to get it right!

Chapter 7
Pain Is Not a Choice,
but Suffering Is...

Suffering ceases to be suffering at the moment it finds meaning.

—Victor Frankl

We are not the wound; we are living in the experience of the trauma, and how we choose to move forward as either a victim, or a victor defines who we are. Accountability is everything!

This means you are owning your part of the experience. Not rationalizing the behavior but instead, leaning into it. In accountability, there are no BUTS... You don't rationalize your actions; you don't blame others or find excuses. You don't reflect on the circumstances without taking away the truth in the experience. Our spirit knows the truth of what we need to grow and evolve our soul. We attract the life experience that can feel like heart wounds. It can hurt and can be challenging to accept, but how we grow from the experience, understanding that there are no accidents, will deliver us from the suffering and into the hands of God for healing.

In order for the light to enter your heart, you can't deny your pain. You can't change what you don't acknowledge. In the matter of light in one's heart, you must understand that the pain lives in your heart and radiates through your body. Emotional pain is like waves of energy, but when transformed into the body, it mirrors physical pain. Releasing emotional pain can be done in different ways.

Imagine holding a tight fist. It begins to hurt, but when you release your fist, there is a sense of relief.

Any experience that leads to the emotion of fear constricts and restricts our heart like a fist. Tears can help us feel a sense of relief and we can find ways to cope with this tension by doing activities such as, yoga, running, and exercise. Be careful not to self-medicate to numb the pain you feel but can't identify. Choose healthy ways to release the deep feelings that fill your emotional body and reflect on the origin of the imbalance that is causing your internal disconnect. This can attract challenging life experiences as our wake-up call looks to change the direction of our life path. We are designed to live in the light, but to do so, we must live in the human experience where we have the opportunity to elevate our spiritual being.

Suffering is a choice; it is an attitude created in the mind, a way that emotional pain can manifest because of the synchronicity of the mind and emotional body.

Emotional pain is like a wave. It has a cognitive beginning, registering in the mind and proceeds into awareness and enters the heart, the center of our emotional body. Suffering is the extension of that wave that can get stuck in one's heart, creating a blockage. It can last a lifetime creating a life of victimization, and a resistance to the natural flow of the light. The light is love; it is God. Suffering blocks the ability to love because suffering is a negative energy where love does not exist. A consequence of this is insecure attachment to others. It becomes difficult to experience authentic love in the here and now because a blockage exists in the heart from a past experience. This is a choice! One can look deep into the emotional pain, learn the spiritual lesson of the experience, understand self-accountability at a deeper level, and not feel victimized because you have a heightened understanding. Suffering can seem like an easier option than feeling accountable for a negative experience, but it has its consequences. Leaning into the pain to have a higher understanding of "why me?" helps eliminate suffering. Choosing to suffer as a victim can create long-lasting emotional pain that impacts one's life, giving another opportunity for the unlearned lesson to revisit. Every experience of love and pain is given to us with purpose to turn to God and feel His love and comfort; and gives us opportunity to grow into our higher spiritual selves. If you can learn the lesson, the suffering will dissipate and you will begin to release the emotional heart blockage, healed by the light to love and be loved authentically. This is what it means to heal the wounded heart and live in the light!

All of life's existence is an act of service with the intention to serve God, not self.

Chapter 8
Choosing Life

I thank God for protecting me from what I thought I wanted and blessing me with what I didn't know I needed.

–Unknown Author

We incarnate with purpose: to have contrasting experiences to spiritually evolve, be emissaries of light, glorify God, and strive to be in His likeness. It is here that we are the teacher and the student, giving and taking from one another to fulfill the promise of purpose in one's life. In the spiritual realm there is unconditional love and perfection created in the eyes of our Creator. It is in the human experience and its challenges that the soul evolves. We have a spiritual desire to purify our souls to be in the image of God. It is through our life experiences that we have the opportunity to grow within. In the contrasts of life, we experience opposites, such as good and evil, happy and sad, light and dark, love and fear, etc.

In the spiritual dimension, there is the absence of opposites because the soul is perfectly created by God in all His magnificence. When the soul incarnates to the human body it strives for the unconditional love of God. When we are in life and separated from God, there is a sense of emptiness. We are born longing for the unconditional love of God from the spiritual realm. If we don't turn to God to fill this emptiness, we tend to self-medicate and temporarily feel full, but this is not the authentic love of God. It is a hole in the soul that only the relationship with God can fill. Often, efforts to fill this emptiness are with drugs, food, sex, attachment to material things, etc. But this leads to dysfunctional behavior, addictions and poor mental health. God's presence in our lives is necessary to feel authentic love and the joy we seek, and to fill the emotional emptiness. Our soul also incarnates for the evolution of generations of one's lineage. We are the guardians of our own life experience, along with our ancestors, spiritual guides, angels and God. We are not victims but participants in the game of life, where we strive to find our purpose, our divine connection, and to embrace our ultimate joy, happiness, love, and salvation. These are reasons we choose life.

Trauma in the Formative Years

From inception our spirit experiences woundedness. From the birth experience into the world, the baby's first emotion is to cry, a disconnect from the womb and heaven. To live is to know trauma! Here, with the first breath of life, the very breath that is the connection to a baby's life journey, it is a mother's love that subsides the pain and separation. The skin-to-skin connection with a mother, mirrors God's love for the baby to know

46

in their first life experience. When there is a lack of love and connection during the birthing process the first emotional heart blockage can be created. Life begins with pain and healing begins at birth. A baby's spirit begins to yearn for the connection of God.

Beginning in utero until the age of 3 is a child's greatest brain development. The 2nd greatest brain development is from ages 3-10. These are the formative years, the years that are the greatest influence on who one will become as an adult and how one will experience self, love, life, loss, attachment, and spiritual connection.

As a child's brain develops, it becomes a working template for all that it sees, hears, feels and experiences. The narrative of the child begins. If the child's needs are met, and they experience love, affection, safety and joy, this child develops secure attachment and tends to thrive in the world. The spiritual connection takes root! If the child's needs aren't met, and there is trauma, grief, loss, loneliness, etc., an insecure attachment develops that often becomes the foundation of future relationships. There is a disconnect to unconditional love, which allows fear, anxiety, avoidance and/or dismissiveness to appear in the personality dynamic of the individual. This has a relational impact on one's life. Self-awareness is necessary before healing and growth can occur and healthy relationships can develop.

God gifted us with a defense mechanism to reject emotional suffering, but at the same time, He wants us to turn to Him in the awareness of it. Although we can be in denial, God hopes we will turn to him for peace and deliverance. Most people of the world work to disconnect/minimize their traumatic woundedness. This does not heal the trauma. Ignoring internal emotional pain created by a traumatic experience allows it to manifest in your body in many ways. The physical is synonymous with pain and trauma and often mirrors what is going on within one's emotional body. Ignoring it only increases the risk for disease to develop, as well as physical issues. We are designed to experience pain and suffering to grow spiritually. Who are you turning to when you are overwhelmed with physical or emotional pain? Are you a victim or is this an opportunity to delve deeper into why you are having this experience? If you don't connect the pain and the experience to the spiritual lesson, you have just missed the opportunity to grow closer to God.

Our emotion is the vehicle that connects us to the light. The emotional body is the home of the soul. It longs to be connected to the Source and God's unconditional love. It's human nature to avoid pain, but without leaning into the pain we live with a lack of authenticity, the reality that's a combination of what we experience and then the perception of that experience. Mental thoughts can compete with one's emotions. The disconnection is when we turn off the emotional valve, so we don't have to feel. This is a common state of being in our world right now. This is what has resulted in a world of isolation and disconnection! Living in community with others is an essential need of humanity. We can pretend to desire separation, but this has proven to lead to depression, sadness, discontent, suicidal ideation and suicide. We are designed to commune together.

The spiritual world, combined with the physical human experience, assists us to evolve in love, forgiveness and mercy, knowing God and to glorify Him. This is the ultimate goal for a spiritual being when having a human experience.

Choosing Our Family Before Incarnating

When our parents/caretakers fail us, it can be challenging to trust that the almighty God can love us. It's so easy to think that if there is a God, why would He choose this family for me? Human woundedness from betrayal, rejection or abandonment can impact our spiritual growth. It becomes more difficult to take that leap of faith in the spiritual world because you may not feel safe in your human experience. When emotional pain exists and there is a risk of investing oneself in someone that may ultimately hurt you, it is challenging to enter healthy loving relationships because you are afraid that your past experiences of betrayal, rejection and/or abandonment can happen again. On some level, you can fear your needs may never be met. One becomes avoidant relationally from fear of not being safe. To trust and become vulnerable emotionally it is necessary to be intimate spiritually. This illuminates the need for forgiveness and the healing of childhood traumas, where secure attachment is necessary to have healthy trusting relationships. In order to release the emotional pain, those wounds that have taken root in your heart, it is necessary for the heart to trust the presence of God's love and His divine light. The light is only a breath away because God's love is always present, but when the heart is filled with toxic energy, there is little room for one to see the light, feel the hope, and embrace God's love. God waits for you to cleanse yourself from your transgressions and traumas with intention and to feel His love that has always been present but often challenging to feel, amidst life's distractions.

Purification is a process in which one releases the shadows and the stories around the feelings of being victimized. The emotional pain must be released from the harbored traumas. They are like waste filling up the spaces in your heart. It doesn't mean you will forget your past, but the pain and suffering are let go. By letting go, you are giving more space for the heart to make room for the light. This process creates a spiritual awakening, a flooding of love and joy that can change the course of your life, as you undeniably know God has begun to heal your heart and fill it with His light and love.

Chapter 9
Sacred Contracts

As a vital part of a larger, universal spirit, we each have been put here on earth to fulfill a Sacred Contract that enhances our personal spiritual growth while contributing to the evolution of the entire global soul.

– Caroline Myss

Sacred Contracts with God:
Understanding Divine Purpose

Throughout human history, people have sought a deeper meaning in their existence, yearning to align with something greater than themselves. The concept of sacred contracts with God offers a framework for understanding this spiritual desire as part of a divine plan. These contracts represent the spiritual agreements or purposes that our souls undertake before entering this life. Rooted in ancient wisdom and spiritual teachings, the idea suggests that our lives are not random but are instead imbued with divine intention.

The Concept of Sacred Contracts

A sacred contract is an agreement between the soul and the Divine, made before birth, to fulfill a specific purpose or mission in this lifetime. This idea is often linked to the belief that every soul is created with a unique calling, whether it is to inspire, heal, create, or learn certain lessons. While these contracts are not legally binding in a human sense, they are considered spiritually binding, guiding the choices, challenges, and relationships we encounter.

Caroline Myss, a leading voice on the subject, explores this idea in her book *Sacred Contracts: Awakening Your Divine Potential*. She describes these agreements as archetypal blueprints that help us understand our spiritual purpose and navigate our lives with greater clarity and intention.

Recognizing Your Sacred Contract

Understanding a sacred contract requires introspection and spiritual awareness. Here are some signs that may indicate you are living in alignment with your divine purpose:

1. **A Deep Sense of Calling**: You feel drawn to certain pursuits or roles that resonate with your inner self. This could be a profession, creative endeavor, or cause that feels uniquely "yours."

2. **Recurring Patterns:** Challenges or themes that keep showing up in your life often point to lessons you are meant to learn or aspects of your contract.

3. **Synchronicities:** Meaningful coincidences may occur, guiding you toward opportunities or people that help fulfill your purpose.

4. **Inner Peace Amid Challenges:** Even when life is difficult, there's a sense of alignment and trust in the divine process.

A sacred contract can also be an agreement with another soul that is written in the spiritual dimension. Relationships formed on the other side purposely come into life together and promise to connect with one another divinely to support, advance, heal, teach, and/or protect the individual by doing, saying, and being in this earthly relationship. This contract is designed before incarnating into one's life to impact this person in an important way. It's an agreement between two or more souls to be in this life together at some point as a divine connection to help direct them toward their purpose. It can be loving or challenging, short or long, yet all sacred contracts are purposefully designed. It can be difficult to explain, but one feels the value and uniqueness of this dynamic relationship, and eventually, when this agreement has been fulfilled; its significance is revealed in some way. (*Sacred Contracts* by Caroline Myss).

54

Sacred Contracts: Awakening Your Divine Potential

The Role of Free Will

While sacred contracts outline a spiritual blueprint, they do not negate free will. The Divine allows space for choice, creativity, and growth. Just as a seed has the potential to grow into a tree, the fulfillment of a sacred contract depends on our actions and decisions. This interplay between destiny and free will is a testament to the balance between divine guidance and human autonomy.

Challenges in Living a Sacred Contract

Fulfilling a sacred contract is rarely without struggle. Obstacles, fears, and distractions can pull us away from our purpose. However, these challenges often serve as catalysts for growth. They remind us to reconnect with our spiritual essence and realign with the Divine.

For example, someone whose sacred contract involves teaching compassion may face situations that test their patience or require forgiveness. These trials refine their character and deepen their understanding of the lessons they are meant to share.

Strengthening Your Connection

To honor your sacred contract, it's essential to cultivate a spiritual practice that deepens your relationship with God. This might include:

1. **Prayer and Meditation:** Creating quiet moments to listen to guidance.
2. **Journaling:** Reflecting on your life experiences and seeking patterns or insights.
3. **Service:** Engaging in acts of kindness and service often brings clarity to your purpose.
4. **Community:** Surround yourself with like-minded individuals who support your spiritual growth.

A sacred contract with God is an invitation to live a life of purpose, meaning, and alignment with the Divine. It reminds us that we are co-creators in a grander plan, endowed with unique gifts and responsibilities. By seeking to understand and fulfill this contract, we not only enrich our own lives but also contribute to the greater good, reflecting God's love and wisdom in the world. In embracing this sacred agreement, we align with our higher selves and experience the profound joy of living in harmony with divine will.

"Our life's mission, or contract, cannot be defined or measured simply by our external life, however. Your purpose is not only your career, hobby or romantic relationship. A contract is your overall relationship to your personal power and your spiritual power."

- Caroline Myss

Chapter 10
Accountability to Your Inner Child

The wound is not my fault, but the healing is my responsibility.

–*Marianne Williamson*

We incarnate into this world to embrace the deliciousness of life. It is a choice! We have a purpose to fulfill and are given the gifts to complete the multiple goals we have committed to while in the spiritual realm. It is here on Earth that we gain the opportunity to grow spiritually. We desire contrast, and only in experiencing difference can we appreciate what is… Can we know beauty without seeing ugly? Can we know joy if we don't know sadness? Only in contrast can we learn to appreciate our experience of life. It is in the joy that we gain strength and hope, but in the more difficult experiences, we have the greatest opportunity to evolve and get closer to God.

When incarnating into our lives, we begin the journey. Our soul knows much more than our mind understands, but divine interventions orchestrate the experiences necessary to bring our mind to a heightened understanding and it begins to link the mind and soul together. Even a baby can have an AHA moment. And so, it begins...

As a child, we grow up in the family we have chosen, to unfold the greatest learning opportunities. Often, this comes with great challenges, and one might think, "Why would I have chosen this?" Remember, in the ethereal world, time doesn't exist. A lifetime here on Earth is a short time to a spirit on the other side and can feel it's well worth the contrasting experiences.

When incarnating into a lifetime, it's essential to have opportunities to learn and evolve your soul to a heightened level. How quickly we forget when we arrive here that we have a purpose, but in time, all individuals will have a choice to commit to their spiritual journey and find the relics one came for or deny the spiritual journey and live life from a human experience. So, can you answer this question? Are you a human being having a spiritual experience, a spiritual being having a human experience? On page 158, there is an activity for you to do to help you answer that question. It is a spiritual mapping (timeline) that can help you to assess your life from a spiritual perspective.

After completing the formative years of your spiritual map, you can look back and assess your life up to that point; did you feel loved, did you experience trauma, and were your physical and emotional needs met? Do you feel you were a victim during those years? How did these experiences sculpt you and your personality to be who you are today? Continue to create your spiritual map up until your current age.

Now, go back and take time to reflect on what you learned from the challenges you had. There are no accidents here; everything comes to teach us a lesson in life and soul. Our character begins to be sculpted from the womb, and all experiences begin to train us to be who we are meant to become, how to fulfill our purpose and be in union with God. These experiences on your spiritual map will show you your challenges and blessings, the very tools needed to support your mission, as well as introduce you to your soul groups, sacred contracts and lessons.

Review the exercises in the appendix and find the one that best fits your need after working on your spiritual map. Complete the assessments/exercises that will help promote your healing.

How are we accountable to our inner child?

Your inner child is the child you once were, yet still lives within you. It is the child who experienced some form of trauma, pain, loss, sadness, and disappointment; The one that believed in magic, promises, and true love; the child that had a dream of who they were supposed to be. This child is the authentic you that sits deep in your body and soul and needs to regain its voice, its joy, and its happiness; the one that reminds you of feelings, thoughts, smells, and sounds and links it all to memories and experiences from the past. This is the child you are most accountable to, the little you that you made promises to that were never forgotten but may have gotten stuffed away and ignored. This child is the one that needs to come out and feel free to find its way back to its adult self. The child that got stuck when life got hard and unsafe and never grew past that stage of emotional development is waiting. Often, our inner child gets locked within the adult it became. This is the child who felt wounded and, as a defense mechanism, turned off the emotional valve so as not to feel the pain but never learned to turn it back on to feel love. This is the inner child that needs to heal. This is the child that each adult is accountable to. It is our adult self that must parent our inner child to feel safe. Then we can successfully fulfill the incomplete stages of development, where trauma occurred, and the inner child became emotionally stuck. It is here that we can know love, trust life and be liberated to grow our inner child and come together as one with our adult self. This is the beginning of knowing self-love and authenticity. It is then that you can be genuine to yourself. No longer do you feel the need to hide from secrets, loss, pain, shame, fears, disappointments, etc. You can lean into those memories and talk about them without emotional hurt, dysregulation, or fear of judgment. This is where vulnerability becomes the hand that brings you to your truth and your greatest strength. Only by embracing all of yourself can you know your true self. Society can influence you to hide from your negative memories and bring shame for that which doesn't meet expectations and falls short of what society, family and friends desire from you. And at the core, this shame can create a perception that God won't love you if you don't meet certain standards. This very shame can keep you from becoming vulnerable and tapping into your power. It doesn't allow you to embrace your authentic self in fear of disappointing others and feeling shameful. Fear will keep you from finding your inner strength and your self-love. Only in self-love can you truly love someone else. Because without authenticity, true love is impossible!

Are you the child that was lied to, taught biases, and/or unhealthy beliefs, shamed and never felt good enough? Was your narrative written, yet filled with challenges that didn't serve your higher self, and you're still struggling to know who you are? Childhood is the foundation where seeds are rooted, but fruit cannot grow with unhealthy soil. Why? Because fruit on your tree can only grow well in truth, authentic love and alignment with spirit.

*See Inner Child exercise on page 153

Chapter 11
Spiritual Warfare

The enemy is not fighting you because you are weak.
The enemy is fighting you because you have a purpose.

—Unknown author

Another important reason for writing this book is because of the spiritual warfare we all endure. Good vs Evil, and Light vs Darkness has existed since Eve defied God in the Garden of Eden. And it will exist until God says enough. We live each day in a spiritual gymnasium, building muscle and strength against the darkness unless one has resigned to the darkness and gone against the Creator's light. Darkness makes many promises and is very alluring to those with an empty mind because the empty mind is Satan's playroom. Being void of a connection to God creates vulnerability to being tempted by the dark energies that surround us. How do you know if you are in the darkness? You have a sense of discontent, revenge, resentfulness, emptiness, needing more, never satisfied, lacking a sense of joy, obsessions, racing thoughts, addictive behaviors and an absence of inner peace. It may feel like exhaustion, confusion, doubting, and/or depression and it can give you false beliefs, lies, nightmares and broken promises. There is a void, where nothing is enough and there is a desire to need more. There is no sense of satisfaction in self or others. The darkness is critical, greedy, lying, and deceitful. Relationships with others lack joy and respect. The darkness is always playing the victim and not accountable. It is drama and chaos. Darkness affects the universe. It lowers the vibrational frequencies between each individual and all of humanity, which is the heartbeat of the universe.

We are not the stars, nor center of the sky,

Not forged in flame where galaxies lie.

Yet here we stand, with eyes that see,

And wonder whispers through you and me.

No claim to rule, no throne, no chart,

But still we beat a fragile heart.

The cosmos vast, in silent grace,

Reflected in the human face.

-RoseMary Cairo

There is a causal relationship between the inner self and the outer world. The greater the light, the higher the vibrational frequency, which creates heightened positivity and a climate of peace. Light casts out the shadow of darkness. In the world of opposites, we must accept the duality of the universe; where there is light there will be darkness. Practicing a form of spiritual discipline, where there is a deliberate intention to connect with God, however you choose, will help achieve casting out the darkness in your life and receiving God's light. We are given free will to choose how we will live this life. By not choosing a path, you are making a choice. Be intentional with your life!

Our planet is changing. It is crying for help; people are polarized, using politics to bring about their deepest intentions. Hatred and fear vs. love has escalated. The planet is getting hotter and getting to the point where one country can destroy the world. Pandemics have instituted deep fear and loss of independence, and threats to the economy are being driven by the governments. Darkness reigns where God is absent. Spiritual warfare is demonstrated in all facets of life. It is the responsibility of humanity to be the emissaries of light to relinquish the darkness. It takes one candle to light up a cave! We must be the candle by conquering the darkness through our relationship with our authentic self and God. There is an immediacy to assess your spirituality to determine what lane your life exists in. Are you in love or fear, darkness or light?

Do you want to change? Is your life journey joyful, peaceful, and fulfilled? This needs to be a priority in one's life now. Time is passing exponentially, and the state of the Earth matters! It is connected to our soul. How do you think we are doing when you look presently at our state of affairs, as well as internationally? We are all connected, and we must understand that our souls matter for our eternal life, the life of our descendants, and the planet we live on!

We must begin by becoming self-aware of the light and darkness that lives within us. Don't deny your emotions. If you have a pattern of discontent, depression, disharmony, and emptiness, these are signs that you are not living in the light. If you are in a constant state of fear, this is where darkness grows. These conditions are often created in the formative years of your life and can be reinforced by the negative experiences created by the law of attraction. If you are in a state of fear, you will attract more experiences to be fearful. It is imperative to get help for past trauma when the trauma is at the center of fearful emotions and paranoia. Being spiritually disconnected from God is at the core of these emotions. What keeps you from embracing the Creator? It is the darkness that has taken up space within your mind, convincing you to deny God. There is no battle to reclaim your light, so become aware and be willing to receive God into your heart, where His love has existed since your soul was created. How deep is your faith? The disconnect you may feel is the darkness that has filled a gap between you and the Creator. In receiving God back into your life and denying the darkness, you will be able to experience peace, contentment, authentic love and joy.

"When I don't feel joy, I know I have taken my eyes off the face of God".

Chapter 12
Forgiveness

Forgive others, not because they deserve forgiveness, but because you deserve peace.

—Mel Robbins

Forgiveness is a concept that humans work through, throughout their lives. To forgive and be forgiven is part of the human and spiritual experience. The more evolved we are the more thoughtful and compassionate we become as we are challenged with the experiences dealing with forgiveness. We become less victimized and focus more on the lessons learned. There is no doubt that forgiveness of self or others can be the most challenging yet most beneficial life experience.

The word forgiveness is inadequate to explain a complex concept. No one deserves to be forgiven; forgiveness is an act of love. Every human being is destined to have to learn to forgive. It is learning to let go of the toxic energy that anchors you to the event(s) of the past and impacts one's life.

When we can't forgive someone, it causes a kind of energetic and emotional blockage in the body. This creates a "stuck vibration" keeping the person energetically tied to the past wound and to the one who caused it. Unforgiveness can show up as; emotional congestion, where emotions get trapped and replayed, like being caught in a loop; Distorted perception, making people over reactive, suspicious, or defensive in new situations; Stress on the heart center, blocking compassion and self-love, leaving feeling of loneliness, emptiness or unworthiness; As well as, disconnection from self, keeping part of ourselves stuck in the past, making it harder to feel whole, peaceful and present.

Forgiveness: A Path to Freedom

Forgiveness is often a key component of healing, but it can be one of the most challenging aspects to embrace. When our hearts are wounded, especially by another person, the hurt can turn into bitterness, resentment, and anger. These emotions, while understandable, can keep us trapped in the pain and prevent true healing from taking place.

Forgiveness is not about excusing or forgetting the harm that was done, rather it is about releasing the hold that the wound has on your heart so it can heal.

Forgiving someone who has hurt you or even forgiving yourself frees you from carrying the burden of that pain and allows you to move forward with a lighter heart. It is a process, not a single act, and it often takes time. But forgiveness can bring profound healing, allowing you to reclaim your peace and emotional freedom.

Are we asking to be forgiven, or do we need to forgive?

The process of asking for forgiveness must come from a place of worthiness to be forgiven. The first step in asking for forgiveness is the awareness of one's wrongdoing, not from a superficial space but from the depth of accountability and admission. This is a vulnerable moment to let down one's defenses and be filled with humbleness and humility. It is painful to admit one's transgressions. Feeling one's pain is the genesis of self-forgiveness and being forgiven.

When we need forgiveness, it is because we have violated someone's space beyond the healthy boundaries of another person. On some level, we have abused the trust given and created an injury in the relationship. The transgression can violate the victim's space physically and/or emotionally, causing a gap between the intended harmony God created between us. In this understanding, we begin the process of being forgiven. We need to open our hearts and remove the veil of guilt and shame, to feel and embrace God's light, appreciate one's worth, and feel connected to purpose. When forgiven, it is of utmost importance to then forgive self. Holding on to the shame will negatively impact life on many levels. This is an important step in forgiveness.

The need to forgive self...

We can begin with the forgiveness of SELF. It is common to self-deprecate, not honor oneself, and cling to false beliefs from formative years, where a lack of self-worth and self-esteem developed. This can be influenced by the aftermath of trauma, having a learning disability, being bullied, having a challenging diagnosis, etc. Feeling different or unloved can create a dislike or even hatred of self. There are many reasons that create the propensity of self-dislike and at some point, one needs to forgive and know that you have the potential to be wonderful and deserving of love, first by oneself. Self-awareness is the first step!

You have been training your whole life to be you! Until you can liberate yourself from the self-angst you are plagued with, you will be challenged to be able to grow to your potential and have the joy and peace you hope for.

Why is forgiveness of others so challenging?

Ego! The ego desires power and fears vulnerability! It is an illusion that we have control over our lives because the ego gives us a sense of righteousness, a desire to be like God, who is the righteous one. Self-righteousness is counterproductive in our search to be one with God and live in His light. The ego does not align with God. In the Ego state, there is a wall between God and self. There is a focus on being victimized, where love and compassion don't exist, but self-retribution breathes. The ego is toxic and pursues the need for approval, worth, power, greed and validation. It is exhausting and continuously stays present in thought and action. In forgiving others, there is a feeling of the surrendering of power over someone else. You fear that in giving up that power, you will reexperience the betrayal again from the individual. We call it the *hook!* You hold the *hook* that the person hangs from, and you have the power to let go or keep them in a state of shame and guilt. Holding the *hook* comes with the delusion that one has power, but it comes at a great cost. It is tied into the memories and emotions from wrongdoing. The way to set this free and live in peace is by surrendering the *hook* and forgiving who was on it. Forgiveness doesn't mean you have to let this person back into your life; that is a choice, but you free yourself from the burden of being a victim, ultimately having the desired inner peace, and to once again be aligned with God.

Steps to True Forgiveness of Others

To begin the journey of forgiveness ....

Don't be a victim.

"What is the lesson that I am learning because of this experience?"

We must acknowledge that all life experiences teach us something we need to better understand about self. Don't be a victim, it is a negative state of being. Instead, validate the hurt, learn what the experience taught and move on...

Identify & acknowledge your hurtful emotions.

"I can only forgive that which I am able to identify and acknowledge."

Don't deny your feelings or repress that which you feel. Validate the feelings, understanding that they are part of the emotional pain. Then, be ready to release these emotions, knowing they will never serve you. Focus on positive thoughts to improve your emotional body and begin feeling the peace you desire.

Forgive yourself and let go.

"Although it felt good to hold onto the *hook*, I know I must let it go to find my inner peace."

Forgive yourself for holding onto the *hook* and the ways this toxicity has impacted your life and relationships. Understand that by letting go, you are giving yourself permission to no longer revisit the emotional pain and can have a sense of peace, which is the result of aligning yourself with God, living in the light and mending your broken heart.

Let go of the need for revenge.

"I see that revenge is a toxic, negative energy. Truth does not have to be validated. God holds the gavel, and I set myself free from the need for retribution."

The motivation for revenge is often fueled by anger, and it is ultimately powered by anticipated satisfaction or enjoyment. A powerful driving force for revenge is the belief that acting out the desire for revenge will provide an emotional release to help us feel better. The ego is at the wheel of your feelings, but this will never get you to the light! In contrast, a negative action creates a negative reaction! Only positive energy will grant positive results. It's a nonnegotiable in the formula of life.

Breathe in compassion.

"I Breathe in compassion and embrace the experience of deeper authentic acceptance."

Living in the now where the dilemma no longer exists is an important reality. You are fully engaged in the present moment, no longer living in the past of affliction. Compassion is a positive vibration that allows us to pivot our energy from being a victim, wanting revenge, and living in a state of fear to transform into love. This may not be to love your transgressor but to be in a state of love, to be able to love yourself and have a deeper connection to your higher self and God. To love another, you must love yourself.

Forgive unconditionally.

"I am ready to forgive without conditions and not waste time looking at the past. I let go and let God!"

To love unconditionally means to forgive and let go without allowing the negative emotions to seep back into your thoughts. It's about being able to surrender all stipulations and move forward without the residue of your hurt and pain impacting your life and controlling your ability for happiness.

Be grateful.

"I am ready to better understand the lesson behind the experience. Sometimes the tough ones are our greatest teachers."

How can you be grateful for a negative experience? How have you grown? What has changed for the positive in your life? Are you a stronger person because of this experience? What can you share with others and pay forward? Are you closer to God and who you are meant to be? Answers to any of these questions can help you to be grateful for the journey you have walked.

Love again.

"I am ready to release the chains that have kept my heart hostage, so I can feel free to love and be loved without fear."

Forgiveness allows one to love again and break down the walls protecting your heart from the past. It means you can live in the present because you have released the negative energy around the pain and created a clean slate, a pathway to move forward to live in the light. In doing this, you can embrace a more positive self, allowing you to trust yourself and others and to be vulnerable, which is necessary to love. In doing this, you are now in a state of positive vibration, not living in fear from the past but committed to being in a loving vibration filled with gratitude in the present.

Steps to True Forgiveness of Self

Accept you have been in denial of the wrongdoings of self. Many of us are experts at self-deception.

Forgiving yourself is a deep and transformative process. It's not about excusing mistakes but about accepting them, learning from them, and moving forward with compassion.

Here are the key steps to true self-forgiveness:

1. *Acknowledge the Mistake*

Denial or avoidance won't help. Be honest with yourself about what happened, what you did, and how it affected you or others. Do not rationalize your behavior. Accepting responsibility is the first step.

2. *Understand the Root Cause*

Reflect on why you acted the way you did. Was it fear, insecurity, pain, or lack of awareness? Understanding the underlying cause can help you grow and prevent future mistakes.

3. *Feel the Emotions, but Don't Dwell*

Guilt, shame, and regret are natural, but don't let them define you. Process your emotions fully, write them down, talk to someone, or meditate, but don't get stuck in self-punishment.

4. *Make Amends Where Possible*

If your actions hurt others, take responsibility. Apologize sincerely, make reparations if needed, and commit to doing better. If direct amends aren't possible, perform acts of kindness to restore balance.

5. *Shift Your Perspective*

You are not your mistakes. Recognize that growth comes from learning, and mistakes are part of being human. Instead of defining yourself by what you did, focus on who you are becoming.

6. *Practice Self-Compassion*

Speak to yourself as you would a loved one. Would you condemn a friend forever for a mistake? Treat yourself with the same kindness and understanding.

7. *Learn and Commit to Growth*

True forgiveness comes with change. What lessons did this experience teach you? How will you act differently moving forward? Make a conscious effort to evolve.

8. *Release and Move Forward*

At some point, you have to let go by releasing negative emotion. Holding onto guilt and shame only drains you. Practice letting go through prayer, meditation and visualization. The true release is the purification of your wounded heart which is ultimately completed in the light of God.

Forgiving yourself doesn't mean forgetting, but it does mean giving yourself permission to grow beyond the past. What part of the process of self-forgiveness feels hardest for you right now?

*See Forgiveness Assessment on page 143.

Chapter 13
The Universal Laws of the Divine

These laws are thought to be intrinsic, unchanging laws of our universe. They are the ordinances of heaven & earth *(Jeremiah 33:25) The Lord says: 'If I have not made my covenant with day and night and established the laws of heaven and earth'....* and in *(Job 38:33) Do you know the laws of the heavens? Can you set up God's dominion over the earth?* They are imminent, infallible laws that govern our universe, the universe God created. Every plant, rock, animal, matter and person are ruled by these laws. They are decrees given by our Creator that are non-negotiable. They exist for all without exception. The more you are aligned to these laws the more positive your life experience will be. These laws are ultimately designed to help us align ourselves with the intentions of the Creator.

#1: The Law of Divine Oneness

"We are all threads woven into the same fabric of existence."

Everyone and everything are interconnected in the world we live in. We are all unified through creation by God. We are manifested by the same Creator which interconnects us all into a divine oneness. When we look at others, we can see a reflection of ourselves. Compassion, empathy, and kindness arise naturally when you recognize others as part of yourself. This law is a vibrational frequency of the highest order.

Divine oneness allows us to choose the energy we transmit into the world and to one another. Positive thoughts create positive actions; negative thoughts create negative actions. It is a law of attraction. Every thought, word, or action affects the whole; separation is an illusion.

The heart is the source of oneness. It is the physical organ that has a spiritual connection to God. This is the organ that connects to Him and lives in the center of the emotional body. This is where the essence of God's language lives. Some think it is the mind that connects to God, but the mind can actually hijack this connection. The brain is connected to our ego-self. The ego-self can't connect to God. This self is the narrative of our life, all the experiences and interpretations of those experiences that our brain holds on to as its reality. We often lock these stories of our lives into our narrative, but they are not of our spiritual self. They are the lessons and opportunities to teach us how to grow into our higher self, the part of us that is connected to our soul that our human life searches for but can only be found at our heart center. The false narratives learned from the hard lessons in life can create the masks worn in relationships where genuine love fails to develop.

The human experience is gifted to us to learn how to be in alignment with these spiritual laws by being open to the lessons and growing from them instead of closing the emotional valve where God connects to each of us through the vibration of love, which only the heart can feel. The way to be aligned with God is through the vibrational field of the heart. A wounded heart defaults to the brain. The pain of the wounded heart is not in the emotion; it is in the restriction of feeling, closing the emotional valve. The mind produces fearful thoughts and physical sensations. We restrain ourselves from feeling, for fear of the pain, and it is this very defensive measure that creates emotional restriction that is created in the mind as fear. Remember fear is the opposite of love. Hence, we are no longer feeling connected to the light.

The heart can be healed at any time. The Source is waiting and always there in abundance. We have a choice to release the restriction and let the light in. To release the restriction, one must focus attention on your heart through mindfulness and breathwork. This is deliberate intention. You can feel the tightness in your chest. Don't go into fear, but instead, give yourself permission to stay focused on the restriction in your chest. Inhale through your nose, feeling God's love and breathe out through your mouth, letting go of your fear. Continue to do this and the restriction will begin to release. You may move into anger or sadness as you release your breath. This is good. It is helpful to be associated with a therapist who does spiritual work and can help you release the pain and fear associated with your memories. *See Box-breathing on page 139.

The enlightened souls that have chosen to be here on this earth as emissaries of light have entered transcendence. They no longer experience the ego-self. They are human beings that have evolved into their higher selves and teach authentic love, having no separation between them and God. Our goal is to live in the light. We are here to learn and evolve through our life lessons, enlightened teachers and faith, which brings us closer to the divine love of God. Imagine a drop of water in the ocean. It seems like its own entity, but it's made of the same substance as the entire ocean. Likewise, each of us are like a "drop" in the vast sea of the Divine.

Practical Application:

Treat others with compassion, even strangers.

- Practice: Before judging, remind yourself: "They are a part of me, expressed differently."
- Example: Instead of reacting in anger to a rude driver, send them silent compassion, reducing collective negativity.

Mindful words and actions.

- Practice: Before speaking or acting, pause and ask: "Will this uplift or harm the whole?"
- Example: Choosing kind words toward a stranger, knowing it creates ripple effects beyond the moment.

Healing relationships

- Practice: If there's conflict, remember your healing benefits them and vice versa.
- Example: Practicing forgiveness frees both of you from the weight of resentment.

Oneness Visualization

- Practice: Imagine a web of light connecting you to everyone and everything.
- Example: When you bless yourself, send the same blessing through the web, magnifying healing energy.

#2: The Law of Energy (Vibration)

"Nothing rests; everything moves; everything vibrates."

According to the law of vibration, every particle in the universe is in constant movement and carries energy; nothing rests. This applies to enormous parts of the universe, like the planets and the stars. It also applies to all matter, such as the chair you may be sitting on and the table where your computer sits. Everything in the universe moves in a circular manner, not only in the physical world but our thoughts and desires move in a unique vibration frequency. Each thought and feeling has its own vibration pattern, and it will combine with those that possess identical vibration patterns, which creates a vibrational match. This is chemistry. Our thoughts are connected to the rest of the universe. Our vibration impacts that which we attract into our lives. Positive thoughts create a higher vibration, and you feel light and effervescent. These emotions fall into the love energy: happy, calm, relaxed, peaceful, joyful, etc. Negative thoughts create lower vibrations. One feels heavy and disconnected. These emotions fall into the energy of fear. They can feel sad, scared, frustrated, anxious, depressed, discontent, etc.

Everything in the world has a vibration. The vibration of the heart is concealed. You must take the leap of faith to believe that this exists to have a heightened understanding of the connection to the Divine. Those who hide from this truth will not be successful on this spiritual journey. There is more to the universe to understand that goes beyond the 5 senses. The 6th sense that the entire animal kingdom thrives on is the sense of vibration. As humans, we have neglected this 6th sense, yet it is vital to understand and implement on your spiritual journey. This is how the guidance center works. It is given by God to help us discern between right and wrong, good and bad, love and deception. Close your eyes and sense how you are feeling. In doing so, you are recognizing the energy you are emitting into the world. Do not forget the importance of how others are also emitting their energy to you. Your energy and emotional state influence your reality. Match the vibration that you want!

Practical Application:

Raise your vibration through intentional action

- Practice: Notice when you feel heavy emotions (fear, anger, guilt).
- Practice shifting these feelings by surrounding yourself with uplifting music, move your body or breathe deeply to raise your vibration.

Intentional Morning Practices
- Practice: Start the day with affirmations or gratitude.
- Example: Saying "I am aligned with peace and joy" sets a high vibrational tone that shapes your day.

Visualize with feeling
- Practice: Imagine your goal and feel the vibration of already having it.
- Example: If you want love, visualize being in a loving relationship and feel the joy now.....this aligns your frequency with attraction.

Energy Check-Ins
- Practice: Ask yourself throughout the day: "Where's my vibration right now?"
- If it's low, choose one small action (a laugh, deep cleansing breath, or kind thought) to raise it.

#3: The Law of Action

"Dreams become real when action joins intention."

The attraction goes into motion when there is action! True creation requires aligned action, not just thought. Manifestation requires movement guided by intuition and divine timing.

Each action provides a different result, which is mostly based on thoughts and emotions. It is imperative to select an action that solely supports one's vision. The actions selected must support your thoughts and dreams, which will help you accomplish your goal.

As you likely already know, the Law of Attraction tells us that like attracts like. It's the boomerang theory. What you put out into the universe is what comes back to you. So, in order to have the things you desire in life, you must work on how to vibrate at the same frequency as the things you are ready to receive. The more general lesson here is that being positive, proactive, and loving attracts more of the same into your life. Meanwhile, pessimism, anxiety, and fear will lead you to generate more negative experiences in all aspects of life. By working to live more positively, even just today, you're already using the Law of Action combined with the Law of Attraction to create a better existence for yourself.

The law of action is the law of choice. Where are your thoughts and actions pertaining to your wounded heart? Do you sit in the lane of fear, feeling sadness, depression, anger, etc.? How long have you been stagnated there? Yes, you need to validate your feelings, but the next step is comprehending the importance of pivoting that energy from the victim to a higher understanding of the lesson. This is designed to bring you to your higher self. Here is where the heart needs to heal. This is where it's a choice on how to move forward in the law of action.

While in a place of victimhood, your heart wounds fester. This is a law of action, but the trajectory spirals into your lower self. One must focus on the positive energy of learning and growing to move towards healing and spiritual growth, where you can feel the divine love of God and the peace that it brings to you. This is the law of action and is important in healing the wounded heart and living in the light of God.

Practical Application:

Don't just dream....move!

- Practice: Follow intuitive nudges and take steps that feel aligned with the life you want to live, the you that you want to be and the goals you want to achieve!

- Example: When inspired, act immediately, even if it's a small step.

#4: *The Law of Correspondence*

"As above, so below; as below, so above."

The Law of Correspondence is directly related to the foundational Law of Divine Oneness. At its core, the Law of Correspondence suggests that there is a harmony, agreement, and connection between the different planes of existence, whether physical, mental, or spiritual. What happens on one level of reality mirrors what happens on another.

The key idea here is that patterns repeat throughout the universe, and that prominent patterns can also be found repeating on a very small scale. Look for patterns in your life and in your thinking and notice how they repeat elsewhere in the world. As you do so, consider the kinds of pattern changes you might be able to make and how this will create change on a large scale.

Key Interpretations:

1. *Microcosm and Macrocosm*

   The universe (macrocosm) and the individual (microcosm) reflect each other.

   For example, the structure of atoms is often compared to the structure of solar systems.

2. *Inner World = Outer World*

   Your external circumstances often reflect your

88

internal state.

If your mind is chaotic or fearful, you may notice more disorder or conflict in your outer life.

3. *Patterns Repeat Across Scales*

Patterns, laws, and structures repeat across different levels of reality, from the smallest particles to the largest galaxies, or from personal behavior to societal trends.

4. *Spiritual Growth*

By understanding yourself (your thoughts, emotions, and patterns), you can better understand the world and vice versa.

Practical Applications:

Self-reflection

- Practice: Use life situations as a mirror to examine your inner beliefs or unresolved issues.

Healing and growth

- Practice: Changing your mindset can lead to real-world changes.

Manifestation

- Practice: Aligning your inner intentions with higher spiritual truths can help bring those intentions into reality.

Use life as a mirror

- Practice: If something is off in your outer world, look within to find the source.
- Example: If you experience recurring conflict with others, reflect on your internal dialogue. Are you being harsh or judgmental with yourself?

The Law of Correspondence teaches that everything is interconnected and reflective. Understanding this helps us see that by mastering our inner world, we influence the outer world and vice versa. It's a tool for gaining insight, balance, and harmony across all levels of existence. It's important to remember that your outer world reflects the patterns of your inner world.

#5 *The Law of Cause and Effect (Karma)*

"Every action, thought, or intention sets a cause in motion that produces a corresponding effect."

Nothing ever happens by chance; every action has a corresponding reaction. Everything you experience is the result of a cause, and everything you do becomes a cause that will generate an effect.

Nothing is random; all reactions come to teach us about ourselves and our journey. Human behavior drives an outcome that we don't necessarily control. We can control our behavior, but the response to that behavior is predetermined by the experience necessary for each individual. This response is created to help us learn and gives us the opportunity to progress to our highest potential.

Understanding this law helps you take ownership of your life. By consciously choosing positive causes, you can shape better outcomes. Remember that every action plants a seed, and every seed brings a harvest.

Practical Application:

- Practice: Be intentional in your choices, because your words, energy, and efforts echo back to you.
- Practice: Pause before reacting, ask:" What effect will this cause create?"

- Practice: Practice kindness and integrity to generate supportive outcomes.
- Practice: Reflect on results in your life: what thoughts or actions might have led me here? Adjust accordingly.
- Example: When things go wrong, ask: "What energy am I putting into the world?"
- Example: You consistently show up on time, treat people with respect and work with integrity, eventually, your reliability brings promotion or new opportunities.

#6: The Law of Compensation

"You receive in portion to what you give"

This Law comes after the Law of Cause and Effect, where blessings come into our lives through various forms, such as gifts, money, friendship, etc.

Essentially, *you reap what you sow, in thoughts and deeds.* This law reminds you to be careful about how you treat others and, indeed, the planet.

If you have anger (lower vibration), then your compensation will exist in a negative vibration. What is your intention? If it is in the lane of love, the compensation will be aligned with loving energy. If it is in the lane of fear (lower vibration), the compensation will be negative, even if, at that moment, it seems positive. Generosity, service, and integrity bring spiritual and material returns. Life returns to you the energy and effort you give.

Practical Application:

- Practice: Give freely with a pure heart, whether time, love, or money.
- Example: Practice random acts of kindness without expectation.
- Example: Volunteer your skills without expecting payment & someone you helped recommends you for a paid opportunity.

#7: *The Law of Attraction*

"What you focus on, you draw into your life.
Energy flows toward the vibration you hold."

This Law introduces things, people, or events into our lives by our actions, thoughts, and emotions. All these thoughts are energies that we use to attract more energy. Like attracts like; your frequency attracts similar frequencies. By producing positive energy, we will attract positive energy. Unfortunately, your negative energy will attract more negative energy. The law brings people with similar interests together. Imagine that when you wake up in the morning, your mood creates a magnetic attraction to all things around you. If you wake up positive, an imaginary positive magnetic shield surrounds you. When you get into your car to leave for work, the magnetic shield begins attracting the positive vibration of everyone around you. Your day is going great! But suddenly, you have a negative thought. The positive magnetic shield turns into a negative shield, and all that good vibration is no longer attached to you. You are now a battlefield of negative vibration from all those having negative thoughts and experiences. From that point on, your day becomes negative. Everything seems to be going wrong. With awareness of the Law of Attraction, you can pivot your energy to a positive thought and begin attracting positive energy again! It is imperative to be intentional.

All living things participate in the love and fear energies. What you emit into the world is what comes back to you. It is like living in a world of mirrors. For this reason, it is important to pivot your vibration to a positive thought to gain a positive response.

Six Steps to shift your vibration from negative to positive.

◆ Turn your focus inward.

◆ Create your place of peace and joy.

◆ Visualize being there and use all your senses when you're there (see, hear, smell, taste, touch).

◆ Being in your place of peace creates positive thoughts and will help you pivot your energy to be positive.

◆ Continue to practice this daily.

◆ Begin to co-create your life.

Practical Application:

Focus on what you desire, not what you fear.

- Practice: Use visualization or scripting to emotionally align with your desired outcome.

- When you begin to feel negative, depressed or sad go through the above steps to pivot your energy from negative to positive and attract positive thoughts, feelings and experiences into your life.

- Example: Instead of saying, "I don't want to be broke," shift to "I welcome financial stability and abundance."

- Practice: Spend 5-10 minutes each day imagining your desired outcome as if it has already happened.

- Example: Picture yourself in the job, relationship, or lifestyle you want. Feel the emotion as if already being there.

- Practice: Speak positive, present-tense affirmations daily to align your energy with your desires.

- Example: I am worthy of love, and it flows freely into my life.

- Practice: Keep a gratitude journal.

- Example: To start your gratitude journal, write 5 things you're thankful for. Every morning add one more thing you're thankful for to your list. Read your entire gratitude list every night before sleeping. Continue this ritual. Gratitude shifts your vibration, making you more magnetic to good experiences.

#8: The Law of Perpetual Transmutation of Energy

"Energy is never still, it shifts, rises, and transforms through you."

The Universal Law states that we possess the power to change the conditions of our lives. Energy is always in motion and can be transformed. Higher vibration consumes and transforms lower ones, and we can change the energies in our lives by understanding the Universal Laws.

The Law of Perpetual Transmutation of Energy states that everything around us is in constant flux. You can't see all these changes because many of them exist at the cellular or atomic level, but they carry on regardless.

The reason that it's so important to be aware of this Law is that it helps you see how you can trigger positive change. Specifically, keep in mind that high vibrations can trigger improvements in low vibrations.

For example, if you're vibrating at a low frequency, exposing yourself to the high frequency of a happy, encouraging friend will naturally trigger energy transmutation in you.

You are not ultimately responsible for other people's feelings, but you can influence their energy through your vibration. Energy is contagious. If you have a higher (positive) vibration, you can help uplift others and vice versa.

Practical Application:

- *Shift stuck energy by doing something creative or active.*

- Practice: When feeling low, shake it off, literally. Dance, walk, or paint to move the energy.

- Example: Ground yourself by going barefoot into the grass.

- Example: Hug a tree! This can support you physically, mentally, and energetically and is backed by science.

#9: *The Law of Relativity*

"Nothing is good or bad until it is compared to something else." and "Everything is relative."

To develop, we must go through a series of problems while remaining connected to our heart. Life's challenges are opportunities for growth and perspective. This law also teaches us that we tend to compare our problems with other people's problems. No matter how difficult and great the situation might be, there will always be someone else in a worse or better position. All things are relative and are compared to appreciate value. Every situation or experience is neutral; it's your comparison or perspective that gives it emotional weight.

People continuously try to compare their lives with others, but from the spiritual perspective, no one's life can really be compared to anyone else's. Each life is unique, and every person comes into this lifetime with a purpose designed specifically for them with the Creator. This is co-creation. Looking at the facets of one's life through a kaleidoscope helps us to see the different perspectives and appreciate, instead of comparing just the beauty or sadness of our life to others. The contrast on all levels is important. Someone may have abundance but have deep depression, another person may be beautiful but have addictions.

Key Principles

1. **Everything "just is" until you compare it.**
No situation is inherently good or bad. It only becomes so relative to something else.

2. **Your problems are not as bad as they seem**. When facing difficulties, the law teaches that others may have harder challenges, helping you see your situation from a more balanced or even grateful perspective.

3. **Growth through contrast.**
You can only recognize strength by comparing it to weakness, success by comparing it to failure, or light by comparing it to dark.

4. **Perspective is power.**
This law teaches that how you interpret your experiences shapes your emotional response, not the experience itself.

Practical Applications:

1. *Shift Your Perspective in Difficult Times:*
   When you're feeling down or overwhelmed, remember that challenges are relative.
   - Practice:
     - Compare your current hardship with a past one you've overcome.
     - Realize your strength and progress instead of focusing on what's wrong.

100

   o Say: "I've handled worse. I can handle this."

2. *Stop the Comparison Trap*:
   Instead of comparing yourself to someone "ahead" of you, compare to where you were a month, a year, or five years ago.
   - Practice:
      o Use journaling: "How have I grown?"
      o Celebrate your own timeline. Everyone's journey is different.

3. *Use Contrast to Cultivate Gratitude*
   Contrast helps you recognize what's good. You can't know light without dark, or joy without sadness.
   - Practice:
      o At the end of the day, list 3 things you're grateful for that you might otherwise take for granted, like clean water, mobility, or a safe home.

4. *Neutralize Emotional Triggers*
   If someone triggers you emotionally, use relativity to take a step back.

- Practice:
  - Ask: "Compared to the big picture, how important is this?" This helps you regulate your emotional response and gain clarity.

5. *Use Relativity to Set Realistic Goals*

   When setting goals, compare only to your own past progress, not others' highlight reels.

- Practice:
  - Track your weekly growth and acknowledge small wins as meaningful steps forward.

Affirmation to Align with the Law of Relativity:

"I choose to see my challenges in context and recognize how far I've come."

#10: The Law of Polarity

"Everything is dual; Everything has poles. Every opposite exists to reveal the value of the other."

This law states that everything has an opposite and those opposites are part of the same whole (hot-cold, light-dark, love-fear). One cannot exist without the other, and movement between poles is always possible.

Change unwanted thoughts by thinking on the opposite pole. Without experiencing the contrasts in life, we can't appreciate its true meaning. In the absence of the opposite, there is nothing. We can't appreciate joy if we don't know sadness. We don't understand healing without woundedness. We can't experience beauty if we don't know ugly.

When thinking about the Law of Polarity, the most important thing to remember is that absolutely everything has an opposite and that the very existence of these opposites allows us to understand our lives.

Consequently, when you go through something difficult, it will be this very challenge that helps you truly appreciate the good developments to come. By regularly reminding yourself of this, you can improve your resilience in troubled times. For example, though a bad break-up is painful, it teaches you what doesn't work for you in a relationship, which ultimately helps you to find the person who does. It is important to embrace contrast as part of divine balance.

Practical Application:

Here are some practical ways to use this law in daily life:

Reframe Challenges

- Practice: When you face a problem, remember there's an opposite side: opportunity, lesson, or growth.

- Ask: "What is the gift or upside hidden in this?"
  Example: If you're feeling rejected, look for how it's freeing you to align with people or paths that truly support you.

Shift Emotional States

- Practice: Emotions are on a spectrum (e.g., sadness $\leftrightarrow$ joy).

- Identify where you are, then take steps, however small, toward the opposite pole (gratitude, movement, connection).

Improve Relationships

- Practice: Recognize that every person has a "light" and "shadow."

- Instead of resisting someone's difficult traits, see how they balance their gifts (e.g., a partner's caution may balance your impulsiveness).

Manifest Desired Outcomes

- Practice: Visualize what you want, then notice where you currently stand on that spectrum.

- Take aligned actions to move gradually toward the desired pole.

Practice Acceptance

- Practice: Because everything contains its opposite, life's "downs" are part of the same continuum as the "ups."

- Acceptance of contrast helps you stay steady, knowing tides shift.

Shift Your Perception.

- Practice: When facing a negative situation, find the hidden good or opportunity.

- Example: When dealing with failure,
  Ask: "What is this teaching me?" or "How can I grow from this?"

#11: The Law of Rhythm

*"Everything flows in and out; all things rise and fall.
Life moves in cycles, flow with the seasons,
not against them."*

All energy vibrates at a certain speed and rhythm. Everything has a cycle and stages of development. The only way to master each rhythm is by facing the negative part of each cycle.

Sometimes called the Law of Perpetual Motion, the Law of Rhythm is (unsurprisingly) focused on movement. In particular, it refers to the fact that all life moves in cycles, seasons, tides, phases.

You can see this in nature, e.g., in the seasons. However, it equally applies to a person's life stages and reflecting on this helps you to gain perspective on the body's aging process.

Today's season may be good, but nothing is permanent, so enjoy what you have while it lasts. Alternatively, perhaps you're in a negative part of the cycle right now, but it may be the very thing that prepares you for a prosperous change in cycles next month.

Understanding your cycle is the first step to having a heightened awareness that this, too, will pass. If you're in a positive cycle, embrace it and enjoy it fully because the cycle will eventually change. If you are in a negative cycle, there is ultimate light. Learn what you can, purify yourself, and prepare for the next cycle. Trust the ebb and flow. Nothing stays still or stuck forever. If death is imminent, you are preparing to enter your last life cycle but your greatest spiritual journey. Sometimes, the greater the pain, the brighter the light.

Practical Application:

Honor your natural cycles.

- Practice; Don't resist life's ups and downs, flow with them.
- Example: If you're feeling low-energy or uninspired, accept the cycle and use the time for rest instead of resisting, knowing your energy will return and your rhythm will rise again.
- Practice: Flow with change instead of resisting it.
- Example: You're in a "quiet season" with less work. Instead of panicking, you rest, reflect, and recharge. Soon after, a new wave of opportunities arrives.
- Practice: Trust Timing.
- Example: Every season serves a purpose.

#12: The Law of Gender

*"Balance the masculine and the feminine within
to create harmony without."*

According to this Universal Law, everything has its masculine (yang) and Feminine (yin) principles. Each individual needs to balance between masculine and feminine energies to become a master. These energies are inseparable and contradictory opposites that attract and complement each other. Balance is always key.

Everything contains both masculine and feminine elements. Masculine qualities are energy, logic, and intellect, whereas feminine qualities are love, patience, and gentleness. There must be a balance between both masculine and feminine. Without feminine, masculine would tend to act without restraint. And without masculine, there will be a failure in action. Both feminine and masculine are dependent on each other.

The Law of Gender has very little to do with biological sex. Rather, it refers to the fact that there are two major types of energy. You can think of them as masculine and feminine, as yin and yang, or as anima and animus.

We all contain a certain amount of energy and must find a way to achieve a balance between both types if we are to live authentically and happily. Think about the role each type of energy appears to play in your life and whether there is an excess or a deficit of either.

In order to fully understand ourselves, we must seek a balance between our feminine and masculine energy. This can be impacted by culture, religion, and ethnicity but the law still remains constant. Each person needs to embrace strength and vulnerability, gentleness and assertion, giving and receiving, etc. If one is off balance, the universe will create situations to pull from the side that is deficit. Balance will always be a driven force pulled into our life experiences.

Practical Application:

- *Balance your energies.* The masculine (logic, action) and feminine (intuition, receptivity) both exist in you. Learn when to activate each.
- Example: In a creative project, use your feminine side to dream and receive inspiration, and your masculine side to take structured action.

Chapter 14
The Path Forward...

What you are is God's gift to you, what you become is your gift to God.

- Hans Urs von Balthasar

From a spiritual context, the Earth is entering into the 5th dimension, "Ascension," which is a higher plane of consciousness characterized by unconditional love, unity, and heightened awareness beyond the limitations of the physical world. To enter 5D Ascension, we must learn that there is no separation between us. We are all connected by the very God force that creates life. This force flows through each and every living thing. Living in the 5th dimension is a way of seeing, feeling, and behaving that respects the divine in all of us. It involves raising your vibration, shedding your ego, and aligning with higher frequencies. It is a new perspective in which denying or disrespecting that life force within each living thing becomes intolerable. In spirituality, the 5th dimension is a multi-dimensional reality where beings can oscillate themselves through the spiritual and physical world. They understand the spiritual laws of the universe. The more aware humanity becomes of each individual's responsibility to align with God's spiritual laws and live in God's light, the faster we will raise the Earth's vibration to thrive in the 5th dimension.

Challenges ahead

We are navigating new chartered waters that can feel fearful but remember that fear is not in the lane of God. Many are stating we are at the end of times. God is using many means to squeeze humanity and guide us back to Him. Since the development of nuclear fusion, the end of the world has been a reality. Our advanced knowledge can be the demise of humanity, such as AI. The world as we know it will be transformed or destroyed, and we are part of the problem or solution. There is an urgency to get right with your soul journey and your connection to our Creator. With technological advances, time and space internationally and cosmically have gotten smaller, and we are interconnected by milliseconds, which creates more danger of extinction of humanity and our planet. Those who don't live in the light will be challenged to destruction. The power of technology, including all social media, such as Facebook, Instagram, TikTok, YouTube, television, messaging apps, podcasts, etc., creates fearmongering and will be the greatest influence on those who can't lean on the truth.

Misinformation is increasingly being misused to create fear in the world by spreading false, misleading, or distorted information that taps into people's deepest anxieties. This tactic plays on our natural tendency to react emotionally to threats, making it a powerful tool for manipulation.

Here are several ways misinformation is being exploited to instill fear:

1. Exaggerating Threats

One common way misinformation is used to generate fear is by exaggerating real or perceived threats. Whether it's a health crisis, social unrest, or economic instability, misinformation often amplifies the danger to make situations appear far worse than they truly are. By presenting extreme or sensationalized versions of events, those who spread misinformation can provoke widespread panic, causing people to react out of fear rather than rational thought. For example, during global health crises like the COVID-19 pandemic, misinformation circulated about the severity of the virus, fake cures, and conspiracy theories about its origins. These false narratives heightened anxiety, leading to distrust in public health authorities and worsening the crisis by influencing harmful behaviors, loss of jobs and medical practices.

2. Creating Divisions and Polarization

Misinformation is also used to sow division and polarization within societies. By targeting specific groups and spreading false or misleading information about them, it can deepen existing tensions or create new conflicts. For instance, misinformation in campaigns may portray certain ethnic, religious, or political groups as dangerous or untrustworthy, stoking fear and hatred.

This technique has been employed in political settings, where fake news and misleading information have been used to discredit opponents or stoke fear about political ideologies. When people are made to believe that a certain group poses a direct threat to their safety or way of life, it creates an atmosphere of fear and distrust, undermining social cohesion.

3. Weaponizing Conspiracy Theories

Conspiracy theories are a powerful tool for spreading misinformation and fear because they often suggest that hidden forces are working against the public's best interests. These theories prey on uncertainty and can lead people to believe in sinister plots, often with little or no evidence. The spread of conspiracy theories is particularly dangerous because it can cause individuals to reject official explanations or expert advice, leading to fear-driven behavior that disrupts society.

What is even more dangerous is not knowing who to believe. It is imperative to research and find the truth, leaning on God for direction and discernment.

4. Exploiting Social Media

Social media has become a fertile ground for the rapid spread of misinformation. The viral nature of these platforms allows false information to reach millions of people quickly, often before fact-checkers can debunk it. Algorithms designed to promote engaging or sensational content often push emotionally charged misinformation to the forefront, increasing its visibility and impact.

This creates a feedback loop where users are more likely to see content that confirms their fears, reinforcing their belief in misinformation. Fearful messages spread faster and more widely because people tend to share information they find alarming, even without verifying its accuracy.

We urge every individual to raise their vibration by connecting to God and casting out evil, the darkness that deceives us through social media, greed, power, artificial intelligence, materialism, and fear.

Chapter 15
God's Word

God's word is the compass in the storm, the light in the dark, and the anchor in the drift. Without it, we wander; with it we walk in truth.

−RoseMary Cairo

Following God's truth in a world filled with misinformation requires discernment, spiritual grounding, and a commitment to seeking authenticity in what you believe and practice. God's word is the ultimate source of truth that transforms and guides us.

Here are some steps to help you stay aligned with God's truth while intentionally avoiding the pitfalls of misinformation and lower vibration:

1. Seek Wisdom Through Scripture

God's truth is often revealed through scripture. Regularly studying sacred texts and involving yourself in spiritual studies can help you stay rooted in divine principles that promote love, justice, honesty, and compassion. Scripture provides a foundation for

understanding what is true and just in God's eyes, helping you filter out misinformation that conflicts with these core values.

•Key verse: "Your word is a lamp to my feet and a light to my path." (Psalm 119:105)

By grounding yourself in scripture, you gain spiritual clarity and insight, enabling you to better recognize misinformation when it contradicts God's teachings.

2. Pray for Discernment

Prayer is a powerful tool for seeking God's guidance. When you feel uncertain about what is true, pray for discernment. Ask God to help you see the difference between truth and falsehood and to give you the wisdom to navigate situations where misinformation may be present. Through prayer, you can invite God's light to illuminate your understanding.

•Key verse: "If any of you lacks wisdom, you should ask God, who gives generously to all without finding fault, and it will be given to you." (James 1:5)

Discernment allows you to be patient, thoughtful, and spiritually attuned rather than rushing to conclusions or reacting impulsively to information.

3. Test Information Against God's Character

When evaluating information, ask yourself whether it aligns with the nature of God. God's truth is consistent with values like love, peace, justice, and kindness. Misinformation often fosters fear, division, hatred, or confusion, which are not reflective of God's nature.

•*Key verse*: "But the wisdom from above is first pure, then peaceable, gentle, open to reason, full of mercy and good fruits, impartial and sincere." (James 3:17)

If information is rooted in manipulation, fearmongering, or divisiveness, it is unlikely to align with God's truth. On the other hand, God's truth fosters harmony, unity, and understanding.

4. Be Humble and Open to Correction

A key to following God's truth is maintaining humility. Sometimes, we may unknowingly believe or spread misinformation. Being humble allows you to admit when you're wrong and to seek correction without letting pride get in the way. Approach conversations with a willingness to learn and a readiness to be guided by God rather than your own assumptions or biases.

•Key verse: "Pride goes before destruction, and a haughty spirit before a fall." (Proverbs 16:18)

Seek the truth with a humble heart, being open to refining your views when presented with new information or perspectives that are more aligned with God's truth.

5. Rely on Trusted, Credible Sources

In a world of misinformation, it's important to carefully consider the credibility of the sources you're relying on. Trusted sources should be transparent, fact-based, and aligned with values of truth and integrity. Avoid sources that are overly sensational and biased without evidence.

•Key verse: "The simple believe anything, but the prudent give thought to their steps." (Proverbs 14:15)

Practicing discernment means looking for facts, cross-checking information, and seeking out multiple perspectives before drawing conclusions. Surround yourself with faith leaders, scholars, and media outlets that demonstrate a commitment to truth.

6. Cultivate a Spirit of Love, Not Fear

Misinformation often capitalizes on fear to manipulate people's emotions and decisions. God's truth, however, brings peace and calm, not panic or terror. When confronted with information that causes fear or anxiety, take a moment to reflect and assess whether it comes from a place of truth.

•Key verse: "For God has not given us a spirit of fear, but of power and of love and of a sound mind." (2 Timothy 1:7)

Fear-based reactions often cloud judgment. When living in God's truth, you operate from a place of peace, empowered by love and clarity rather than fear and confusion.

7. Engage in Community and Dialogue

God calls us to live in a community where we can learn from each other and support one another in seeking truth. Engage with a faith community that values open dialogue and critical thinking, where you can discuss difficult issues, challenge misinformation, and grow in understanding together.

•Key verse: "As iron sharpens iron, so one person sharpens another." (Proverbs 27:17)

Conversations with trusted spiritual mentors or fellow believers can help you discern the truth and avoid falling into the traps of misinformation. Be open to sharing what you've learned while also being willing to listen and learn from others.

8. Act in Truth and Integrity

Following God's truth means embodying honesty and integrity in your actions. It's important not only to seek truth but also to live it. Resist the temptation to spread unverified information, even if it aligns with your beliefs or emotions. When in doubt, remain silent or take the time to investigate further before sharing or acting on questionable information.

- Key verse: "Therefore each of you must put off falsehood and speak truthfully to your neighbor, for we are all members of one body." (Ephesians 4:25)

Living in integrity means committing yourself to truth, both in what you believe and in what you share with others. Following God's truth in a world filled with misinformation requires patience, wisdom, and a deep connection to God's guidance. By staying grounded in scripture, praying for discernment, testing information against God's character, and seeking out reliable sources, you can navigate through confusion and avoid falling prey to falsehoods. Ultimately, God's truth brings peace, clarity, and love, while misinformation sows fear and division. Trust in God's light to guide you as you seek to live in truth with a heart centered on faith and integrity.

Chapter 16
The Connection Between God and Your Emotions

"God is not distant from our emotions; He meets us in them. In joy, He celebrates with us. In sorrow, He comforts. In anger, He listens. Our feelings are not foreign to God; they are a doorway to a deeper relationship with Him."

–RoseMary Cairo

The connection between God and your emotions is profound, often working beneath the surface of our everyday awareness. Emotions are part of our human experience, shaping how we navigate the world and how we respond to life's challenges. Yet, within these emotions lies a sacred thread that ties us to the Divine, a connection that invites us to understand our feelings as more than mere reactions but as reflections of our spiritual journey.

Emotions as Divine Signals

In many spiritual traditions, emotions are seen as signals from the soul or spirit, guiding us toward greater self-awareness and connection with God. When we feel joy, peace, or love, we can interpret these emotions as glimpses of divine presence. They are moments when we align with God's essence, tapping into the profound sense of harmony that comes from living in accordance with divine will.

Similarly, negative emotions such as sadness, anger, or fear are not meant to be shunned or repressed but rather understood as part of the process of spiritual growth. These feelings often arise when we are out of alignment with our true selves or with God's purpose for our lives. They may signal a need for change, reflection, or healing, serving as catalysts for deeper spiritual work. Put focus towards greater self-awareness, have a heightened understanding of your emotions and then pivot your negative energy to be positive.

The Role of Love and Compassion

At the heart of the connection between God and our emotions is the experience of love and compassion. Many people describe feeling closest to God in moments when they are overwhelmed by love, whether through relationships, acts of kindness, or simply being in awe of the beauty of life. Love is often seen as the most direct reflection of God's presence within us. In Christian teachings, for example, the commandment to "love your neighbor as yourself" is rooted in the belief that God is love itself.

Compassion, too, deepens this connection. When we feel empathy for others or for ourselves, we tap into a divine quality that transcends personal boundaries. In these moments, we are not merely feeling for another person, we are sharing in the divine love that God has for all creation. Compassion helps us see the world through God's eyes, allowing our emotions to become a bridge between heaven and earth.

Prayer and Emotional Transformation

One of the most powerful ways to experience the connection between God and your emotions is through prayer. Prayer is not just a request for intervention or a ritual; it is a conversation with the Divine, an opportunity to open your heart and soul to God's presence. When we pray, we bring our emotions into the light of God's love, allowing them to be transformed.

In times of distress or confusion, prayer can help shift our perspective. It allows us to release the burdens we carry and place them in God's hands, trusting in divine wisdom to guide us. Similarly, in moments of joy, prayer becomes a way of expressing gratitude, deepening our sense of connection with the divine source of all goodness.

Through prayer, emotions that once seemed overwhelming or isolating can become pathways to spiritual clarity. When we surrender our feelings to God, we often find the emotions themselves are transformed. Anger can give way to forgiveness, fear can be replaced by trust, and sorrow can be lifted into peace. In this way, prayer becomes not just an act of faith but a means of emotional healing.

Emotional Honesty and Spiritual Growth

Living in connection with God requires emotional honesty. We cannot truly grow spiritually if we are not willing to face and acknowledge our emotions, no matter how uncomfortable they may be. God invites us to bring all of our feelings, our joys, our pains, our hopes, and our fears into the light.

By embracing emotional honesty, we invite God into the messiness of our human experience. This honesty allows for deep transformation, as it opens the door to greater understanding, healing, and alignment with divine purpose. It is through this process that we learn to trust our emotions as guides, rather than obstacles, on our spiritual journey.

Emotions as a Reflection of God's Presence

Ultimately, the connection between God and our emotions remind us that we are not alone in our feelings. Every emotion, whether positive or negative, can serve as a reflection of God's presence within us. Our feelings are part of the divine tapestry of life, a way for us to experience the depth of our humanity and our connection to something greater.

When we see our emotions in this light, we begin to understand that God is with us in every moment, in our laughter and in our tears, in our fear and in our courage. By embracing our emotions as sacred, we allow ourselves to live more fully in God's presence, trusting that every feeling, no matter how fleeting, is part of the greater journey toward spiritual wholeness.

In this way, the connection between God and your emotions is not just an abstract idea but a lived experience. It is an invitation to engage with your feelings in a deeper, more meaningful way, knowing that through them, you are always connected to the Divine.

Chapter 17
Transforming Emotional Wounds into a Higher Spiritual Relationship with God

Spirituality is recognizing and celebrating that we are all inextricably connected to each other by a power greater than all of us and that our connection to that power and to one another is grounded in love and compassion. Practicing spirituality brings a sense of perspective, meaning and purpose to our lives.

–Brené Brown

Emotional wounds, while are often sources of deep pain and suffering, have a unique ability to draw us closer to God. In moments of vulnerability and brokenness, we find ourselves more open to spiritual truths that might otherwise remain hidden. These wounds strip away layers of self-reliance, pride, and illusion, exposing our innate need for divine connection and guidance. Through this process, pain can become a bridge, transforming our weaknesses into avenues for divine strength.

When we bring our wounds before God, they become pathways to a relationship grounded in humility and trust. Rather than seeing God merely as a source of blessings, we begin to understand Him as a healer and companion in our struggles. This shift allows us to see our suffering not as punishment but divinely

orchestrated to draw us into a more authentic, resilient faith.

The journey of healing our emotional wounds with God is not passive. It calls for active faith, self-reflection, forgiveness, and surrender. These wounds, then, are transformed into catalysts for spiritual growth, helping us to cultivate empathy, patience, and compassion for ourselves and others. They remind us that God is not only present in moments of joy but is intimately close in our suffering, helping us rebuild our hearts in alignment with His will.

In surrendering our pain and accepting God's presence within it, we achieve a higher level of spiritual intimacy, one marked by trust, gratitude, and a deep sense of peace. Ultimately, our emotional wounds, when viewed through the lens of faith, become instruments of divine purpose, bringing us into a closer, more resilient relationship with God. Our emotional wounds, painful as they may be, are far from wasted in the context of our spiritual growth. Instead, they serve as powerful tools for transformation and deeper

connection with the Divine.

Here are a few ways in which emotional wounds contribute to our spiritual development:

1. Cultivating Empathy and Compassion:

When we experience emotional pain, it often deepens our empathy for others who suffer. This connection allows us to view others with greater compassion and understanding, which are key elements in most spiritual teachings. Our wounds can make us more attuned to the struggles of others, creating a sense of unity and love that fosters spiritual growth.

2. Strengthening Faith and Surrender:

Emotional wounds challenge our sense of control and force us to acknowledge our limitations. In these vulnerable moments, we often reach out to a higher power, learning to trust in something greater than ourselves. This surrender becomes a vital component of faith, allowing us to place our burdens with God and fostering a deeper, more resilient spiritual relationship.

3. Fostering Humility and Self-Awareness:

Wounds often bring to light aspects of ourselves that we may prefer to ignore or avoid. They push us to confront our weaknesses, fears, and insecurities. This honest self-examination can foster humility, reminding us of our shared human condition and the need for continuous personal and spiritual development.

4. Transforming Suffering into Purpose:

Emotional wounds have a unique ability to become sources of purpose and meaning. Through healing and reflection, many people discover a calling to help others who face similar struggles, turning their suffering into a source of strength. This transformative journey can help us see our pain as a sacred part of our story, allowing us to embrace it as part of a larger purpose within our spiritual path.

5. Encouraging Forgiveness and Release:

Carrying emotional wounds often involves dealing with past hurts and grievances. In seeking healing, we are often called to forgive others, ourselves, or even situations we cannot control. This process of forgiveness not only releases us from the weight of resentment but also frees our spirit, opening space for peace and spiritual clarity.

6. Experiencing Divine Love and Healing:

Through the process of addressing our wounds, we often experience a profound sense of divine love and healing. When we bring our pain into our spiritual practice, we learn that we are accepted, loved, and valued even in our most broken states. This unconditional divine love affirms our worth and opens us to a more profound relationship with the sacred.

In these ways, emotional wounds are not wasted but rather serve as catalysts that deepen our spiritual journey. They draw us closer to divine wisdom, refine our character, and reveal insights that might otherwise remain hidden. By embracing the growth that can come from pain, we allow our wounds to become sacred teachers, guiding us toward greater compassion, resilience, and spiritual awakening.

7. Reconnecting with Yourself

Healing the heart is also about reconnecting with yourself. When we are wounded, we often lose touch with our sense of self-worth, our inner joy, and our purpose. Part of healing involves nurturing your spirit and rediscovering what makes you feel alive, loved, and whole.

This might mean engaging in self-care practices, exploring creative outlets, or spending time in nature. It may also involve reflecting on your values, setting boundaries, or practicing mindfulness and meditation. Reconnecting with yourself means treating your heart with the same compassion and care you would offer to someone else in pain.

8. Embracing Faith and Spirituality

For many, faith and spirituality are powerful sources of comfort and healing. Belief in a higher power and spiritual practices can provide a sense of hope, purpose, and strength amid emotional pain. Trusting that there is meaning beyond the hurt, that healing is possible, and that you are being guided through the process can help ease the burden of carrying a wounded heart.

Spiritual practices such as prayer, meditation, or reading sacred texts can bring peace and perspective. Many find that in surrendering their pain to a higher power, they can release control and find solace in the belief that healing will come in due time.

9. Finding Meaning and Growth in the Wound

While no one wishes for emotional pain, wounds can be a source of growth and transformation. Healing a wounded heart often leads to greater self-awareness, resilience, and empathy for others. The process teaches you about your own strength, your capacity to endure, and your ability to find beauty in brokenness.

Many who have healed from deep emotional wounds go on to help others, offering their wisdom and compassion to those who are suffering. In this way, the wound becomes not just a source of pain but a path to a greater purpose and connection with the world.

Chapter 18
God's Light and the Wounded Heart as Your Strength

Come to God for your healing. Don't hesitate.
God, who is so full of goodness and supply, is always willing to bless, preserve, heal and restore you.

–Joseph Prince

It is often said that our greatest strength comes from our deepest wounds, and when we allow God's light to touch the broken places within us, healing and transformation can occur. Life has a way of leaving scars; emotional, physical, and spiritual. These wounds, however, are not meant to define us or limit us; rather, they have the potential to become sources of profound strength and grace when we allow God's light to illuminate them.

God's Light as a Healing Force

Amid the suffering, it is easy to feel abandoned or lost. But God's light is always present, even when we cannot see or feel it. In times of darkness, we are often called to trust in a power beyond our understanding, a light that transcends the pain we are experiencing. This divine light does not erase the wounds, but it has the power to transform them.

God's light is a source of healing. When we open our wounded hearts to this light, we allow God's love to flow into the places that hurt the most.

The Gift of Brokenness

To live in the light is to recognize that our wounds are not burdens to be hidden but gifts to be embraced. When we allow God's love to penetrate our pain, we realize that every scar has a story, every crack a history that has shaped who we are. These wounds do not diminish us; they expand our capacity for empathy, for love, and for grace.

Brokenness becomes a gateway to transformation when we choose to surrender it to God. What once felt like an unbearable weight becomes the very thing that makes us strong. Through God's healing presence, we learn that our scars are not symbols of failure but of endurance, of having walked through the fire and emerged with a heart healed and still open to love.

Being in the Light

Being in the light means choosing to see our lives through the lens of divine love, even in the face of difficulty. It means trusting that no matter how deep the wound, there is always hope for healing, always the possibility of renewal. Walking in the light is a practice of faith, an acknowledgment that while we may not always understand the purpose of our pain, we trust that God's light is always at work, bringing love where there once was only hurt.

In the end, living in the light and being strong in your wounded heart is not a destination but an ongoing journey. It is about embracing each moment with love, compassion, and authenticity. This path invites us to look inward, quiet the noise of the outside world, and trust the wisdom that arises from within. By letting God's light in, you can cultivate a heart-centered way of being, where we connect more deeply with ourselves and with others, creating a ripple effect of kindness and understanding. The heart becomes an intuitive guide, gifted by God, leading us to live a life of purpose, peace, and genuine fulfillment. This is where true happiness resides.

When we live in the light, we no longer define ourselves by our wounds but by our strength. Living in the light is where the ultimate love and healing exist. It is here where you will find God's love. Come join us as the emissaries of light! We are the difference makers, the solution to the ultimate healing of humanity and the world, one person at a time. It only takes one candle to light up a cave. *Be the candle..........*

Chapter 19
Embracing the Light.... Strength Beyond the Wounds

A mosaic is made of broken pieces, yet it still becomes a masterpiece. In the same way, a broken heart, when placed in God's hands, can be transformed into strength & beauty.

–RoseMary Cairo

Healing the wounded heart is a journey that requires time, patience, and care. It is not a linear process, and there will be moments of progress as well as setbacks. However, with each step toward healing, through grieving, forgiveness, seeking support, and spiritual connection, the heart begins to mend. Over time, the pain softens, and in its place grows a deeper understanding of yourself, a renewed sense of hope, and the capacity to love again.

Though the scars may remain, they can serve as reminders of your resilience and your journey toward wholeness. Healing is possible, and with it comes the opportunity to embrace life fully once again, with a heart that has learned to find strength even in its wounded places.

As we close, we are reminded of the profound truth that, even in our darkest moments, healing is possible through the transformative power of divine light. This journey has shown us that our wounds, while painful, are not destinations but invitations to grow, connect, and experience the depth of God's love. God's light reaches the innermost corners of our being, illuminating the path to forgiveness, resilience, and peace. It teaches us that while pain is a part of our human experience, it does not define us. When we open our hearts to God's presence, we find that each scar can be a testament to His love, each struggle a step toward strength, and each healing a glimpse of His grace.

Healing is a sacred, often gradual journey. It requires us to surrender our burdens, to trust, and to allow divine light to work within us. This book has explored the ways God's light enters our lives, softening the hardened places, restoring hope, and inspiring us to forgive both ourselves and others.

As we step forward, may we carry with us the understanding that God's light is always available, ready to mend our wounds and guide us towards wholeness! With open hearts, we find that healing is not only a possibility but a promise, fulfilled each time we allow God's love to shine through. The journey of healing may never truly end, but with the light of God, we are equipped to walk forward with love, courage, and compassion, while finding strength in our wounded hearts and being forever touched by His grace.

Appendix

#1 Box Breathing

Take a deep breath through your nose and inhale while counting for 4 counts (1-2-3-4). Then, hold for 4 counts (1-2-3-4). While inhaling, focus on God's light and love coming from above and entering your crown and into your heart. Then exhale through your mouth, counting for 4 counts and holding for 4 counts, focusing on letting go of negative energy.

*Repeat this a minimum of three times.

#2 Spiritual Assessment

Spirituality Assessment

Please indicate your level of agreement to the following statements by circling the appropriate number that corresponds with the answer key.

Key:
1. **Strongly agree**
2. **Disagree**
3. **Mostly disagree**
4. **Mostly agree**
5. **Agree**
6. **Strongly Agree**

1. I find meaning in my life experiences.	1 2 3 4 5 6
2. I have a sense of purpose.	1 2 3 4 5 6
3. I am happy about the person I am becoming.	1 2 3 4 5 6
4. I see the Divine in my everyday life.	1 2 3 4 5 6
5. I have a sense of how God/a higher power is working in my life.	1 2 3 4 5 6
6. I feel that there are no coincidences in life.	1 2 3 4 5 6
7. I look for signs in my life that have divine meaning.	1 2 3 4 5 6
8. God's/a higher power's presence feels real to me.	1 2 3 4 5 6
9. I feel I am spiritually guided in my life to fulfill my purpose.	1 2 3 4 5 6
10. I trust my intuition as divine guidance.	1 2 3 4 5 6
11. From day to day, I feel God/a higher power is with me.	1 2 3 4 5 6

12. I feel that God/a higher power listens to my prayers.	1 2 3 4 5 6
13. I believe there is a connection between all things that I cannot see but can sense.	1 2 3 4 5 6
14. I believe in God/a higher power.	1 2 3 4 5 6
15. My faith in God/a higher power helps me cope during challenges in my life.	1 2 3 4 5 6
16. I trust my journey in life and feel it is divinely guided.	1 2 3 4 5 6
17. I do my best to learn the lessons within life's challenges.	1 2 3 4 5 6
18. My spirituality gives me inner strength.	1 2 3 4 5 6
19. Spending time meditating/praying is a constructive use of my time.	1 2 3 4 5 6
20. I feel gratitude in my life.	1 2 3 4 5 6

Scoring the Assessment

Add up your points. The highest score in the spiritual assessment is 120 points. The closer you are to 120 points, the higher you score in your level of spirituality.

#3 Forgiveness Exercise

Sit in a comfortable position, begin by closing your eyes, helping you to look within your emotional body and begin doing the box breathing exercise. (Exercise #1)

Surrender to your breath, release the tension and open up to flush away the negative emotions. Holding a pillow to your chest can help create pressure to release some of these negative emotions you are feeling. Now, you are honoring your emotions instead of restricting them, reducing their power over you. In the acceptance, you honor your feelings and allow them to dissipate and transform the negative energy into a peaceful, more positive vibration. Repeat to yourself a positive affirmation such as "I embrace all my feelings and validate my experience. I am complete and feel the connection to the light of God, which lives within me."

#4 Forgiveness Assessment

<u>Heartland Forgiveness Scale</u>

Directions:

In the course of our lives, negative things may occur because of our own actions, the actions of others, or circumstances beyond our control. For some time after these events, we may have negative thoughts or feelings about ourselves, others, or the situation. Think about how you typically respond to such negative events. Next to each of the following items, write the number (from the 7-point scale below) that best describes how you typically respond to the type of negative situation described. There are no right or wrong answers.

Please be as open as possible in your answers.

1	2	3	4	5	6	7
Almost Always			More Often		Almost Always	
False of Me			True of Me		True of me	

_____ 1. Although I feel badly at first when I mess up, over time I can give myself some slack.

_____ 2. I hold grudges against myself for the negative things I've done.

_____ 3. Learning from bad things that I've done helps me get over them.

_____ 4. It is really hard for me to accept myself once I've messed up.

_____ 5. With time I am understanding myself of the mistakes I've made.

_____ 6. I don't stop criticizing myself for negative things I've felt, thought, said, or done.

_____ 7. I continue to punish a person who has done something that I think is wrong.

_____ 8. With time, I am understanding of others for the mistakes they've made.

_____ 9. I continue to be hard on others who have hurt me.

_____ 10. Although others have hurt me in the past, I have eventually been able to see them as good people.

_____ 11. If others mistreat me, I continue to think badly of them.

_____ 12. When someone disappoints me, I can eventually move past it.

_____ 13. When things go wrong for reasons that can't be controlled, I get stuck in negative thoughts about it.

_____ 14. With time, I can understand the bad circumstances in my life.

_____ 15. If I am disappointed by uncontrollable circumstances in my life, I continue to think negatively about them.

_____ 16. I eventually made peace with bad situations in my life.

_____ 17. It's really hard for me to accept negative situations that aren't anybody's fault.

_____ 18. Eventually, I let go of negative thoughts about bad circumstances that are beyond anyone's control.

HFS Scoring Instructions

Four scores are calculated for the Heartland Forgiveness Scale (HFS):

Total HFS (items 1-18)

HFS Forgiveness of Self subscale (items 1-6)

HFS Forgiveness of Others subscale (items 7-12)

HFS Forgiveness of Situations subscale (items 13-18)

To score the HFS:

1. Scores for items 1, 3, 5, 8, 10, 12, 14, 16, & 18 are the same as the answer written by the person taking the HFS.

Scores for items 2, 4, 6, 7, 9, 11, 13, 15, and 17 are reversed. For example, an answer of 1 is given a score of 7 and an answer of 7 is given a score of 1. Refer to the tables below for more information about scoring individual items.

2. To calculate the Total HFS, **HFS Forgiveness of Self**, **HFS Forgiveness of Others**, and **HFS Forgiveness of Situations**, sum the values for the items that compose each scale or subscale (with appropriate items being reverse scored).

Scores for the Total HFS can range from 18 to126. Scores for each of the three HFS subscales can range from 6 to 42.

Scoring

Items 1, 3, 5, 8, 10, 12, 14, 16, & 18

Person's Answer	Item Score
1	1
2	2
3	3
4	4
5	5
6	6
7	7

Reverse-Scoring

Items 2, 4, 6, 7, 9, 11, 13, 15, &17

Person's Answer	Item's Score
1	7
2	6
3	5
4	4
5	3
6	2
7	1

Interpreting HFS Scores

The Heartland Forgiveness Scale (HFS) is an 18-item, self-report questionnaire designed to assess a person's dispositional forgiveness (i.e., one's general tendency to be forgiving), rather than forgiveness of a particular event or person.

The HFS consists of items that reflect a person's tendency to forgive him or herself, other people, and situations that are beyond anyone's control (e.g., a natural disaster).

Four scores are calculated for the HFS. There is a score for the Total HFS and a score for each of the three HFS subscales (**HFS Forgiveness of Self** subscale, **HFS Forgiveness of Others** subscale, and

HFS Forgiveness of Situations).

Scores for the Total HFS can range from 18 to 126.

Scores for the three HFS subscales can range from 6 to 42.

Total HFS

One's score on the Total HFS indicates how forgiving a person tends to be of oneself, other people, and uncontrollable situations. Higher scores indicate higher levels of forgiveness, and lower scores indicate lower levels of forgiveness.

- **A score of 18 to 54** on the Total HFS indicates that one is usually unforgiving of oneself, others, and uncontrollable situations.

- **A score of 55 to 89** on the Total HFS indicates that one is about as likely to forgive, as one is not to forgive oneself, others, and uncontrollable situations.
- **A score of 90 to 126** on the Total HFS indicates that one is usually forgiving of oneself, others, and uncontrollable situations.

HFS Subscales

One's score on the three HFS subscales indicate how forgiving a person tends to be of oneself (HFS Forgiveness of Self), other people (HFS Forgiveness of Others), or situations beyond anyone's control (HFS Forgiveness of Situations). Higher scores indicate higher levels of forgiveness, and lower scores indicating lower levels of forgiveness.

- **A score of 6 to 18 on *HFS Forgiveness of Self, HFS Forgiveness of Others*, or *HFS Forgiveness of Situations*** indicates that one is usually unforgiving of oneself, other people, or uncontrollable situations, respectively.

- **A score of 19 to 29** indicates that one is about as likely to forgive as to not forgive oneself, other people, or uncontrollable situations, respectively.

- **A score of 30 to 42** indicates that one is usually forgiving of oneself, other people, or uncontrollable situations, respectively.

150

Citing the HFS

The Heartland Forgiveness Scale (HFS) was first developed in 1998, and the current version was finalized in 1999. In 2003, the HFS was published in Positive Psychological Assessment: A Handbook of Models and Measures in a chapter by Laura Y. Thompson and C. R. Snyder. In 2005, Thompson et al. published an article in the Journal of Personality. The 2005 article included the HFS and a series of six studies regarding the psychometric properties of the HFS. Either source can be cited for the HFS.

HFS Citations

Thompson, L. Y., & Synder, C. R. (2003). Measuring forgiveness. In Shane J. Lopez & C. R. Snyder (Eds.), Positive psychological assessment: A handbook of models and measures (pp. 301-312).

Washington, DC, US: American Psychological Association.

Thompson, L. Y., Snyder, C. R., Hoffman, L., Michael, S. T., Rasmussen, H. N., Billings, L. S.,

Heinze, L., Neufeld, J. E., Shorey, H. S., Roberts, J. C, & Roberts, D. E. (2005). Dispositional forgiveness of self, others, and situations. Journal of Personality, 73, 313-359.

#5 *The Bubble Exercise for Forgiveness*

- ❖ Find a quiet place and get into a comfortable position.
- ❖ Close your eyes and think of someone you want to forgive.
- ❖ Imagine you are entering a bubble. In this bubble, you are completely safe. Nothing can harm you physically, emotionally or spiritually.
- ❖ Continue to think of the person you want to forgive.
- ❖ Now imagine that person as a small child and invite them into your bubble.
- ❖ What do you see?
- ❖ What does this person look like?
- ❖ What is their life like?
- ❖ Sit down with him/her. Look into their eyes and connect with this person.
- ❖ Can you hug him/her?
- ❖ Can you feel that you can forgive him/her?
- ❖ If so, imagine hugging this child.
- ❖ Now, let the child go and step out of the bubble when you are ready.
- ❖ This is the beginning of forgiveness and healing.

#6 *The Inner Child Visualization*

❖ Prepare to go on a journey as you engage yourself in pure relaxation, connect with your senses, with yourself and your inner child.

❖ Find a place where you will not be disturbed and turn off all electronic devices.

❖ Remember, this is your time, a chance to escape from your everyday problems, to allow the tensions of the day to disappear and connect with your inner child. (It can be beneficial to record these steps and then play them back as you do this visualization.)

1. Close your eyes.

2. Breathe deeply and slowly through your nose and then slowly exhale through your mouth, allowing any tension within you to melt away.

3. Inhale again, breathing slowly through your nose to the count of four. Feel the air entering your lungs and expanding your diaphragm.

4. With your lungs now full, hold your breath for two seconds and then release slowly on the count of four.

5. Continue this cycle of breathing. Breathe in on the count of four, then hold for two, and breathe out, releasing on the count of four.

6. Continue this breathing cycle for one minute. Take your time to really engage in this

breathwork. Remember, as you breathe out you want to release all tensions in your body.

7. Now, breathe normally, acknowledging that your body feels more relaxed. Your arms and legs will start to feel heavier; you should feel the back of the chair or whatever is supporting your body as you let all the tension go.

8. Imagine now that you can see your favorite place, a place where you truly feel comfortable, safe, free, and relaxed. This place might be a beach setting, forest, garden, your backyard or possibly your bedroom, wherever you feel peaceful and comfortable.

9. In your mind's eye, see this place. It's calling out to you.

10. Walk towards this place now, look around, what do you see here? What's around you?

11. Keep moving closer to this special place and see what is there.

12. Look and see a faint outline of a small child in the distance. Continue to walk closer to this child. You notice that this child looks familiar to you, and you feel compelled to move closer. As you get near, you see this child looks like yourself but a smaller you, a younger you. This is your inner child.

13. What does he/she look like?

14. See what he/she is doing?

15. You get close to your inner child now, and you reach out and say hello.
16. Ask your inner child if you can spend some time together.
17. At this point, respect your inner child's wishes. If he/she needs to be alone, respect the need to be apart, and just be happy with your inner child even from a distance.
18. Maybe your inner child is happy to be close to you. If that is the case, feel free to move closer.
19. Sit with your inner child.
20. Look at your inner child & see where he/she is looking.
21. Look in the same direction, just like seeing through your inner child's eyes. See what your inner child sees, hear what he/she hears, and feel what your inner child feels.
22. Now, as you connect with your inner child, how does it feel to be reconnected to your inner child? What are his/her favorite things to do? What worries or concerns does your inner child have? What are his/her fears? Remember that no fear or concern is too small. Encourage your inner child to talk openly to you.
23. As you listen with your open heart and mind, take several minutes to simply be with your inner child.

24. As you continue to listen to your inner child with your heart, ask if there is anything he/she may want or need from you.

25. Give your inner child the opportunity to communicate with you in any way he/she feels most comfortable. Maybe he/she will communicate with you by drawing a picture, speaking openly with you, singing to you, or possibly even communicating in silence. Encourage him/her to be comfortable with you in the next moments.

26. If your inner child wants something from you, and you can give it, go ahead and give this to your inner child.

27. Possibly, he/she just wants to be held, if so, give your inner child a hug. If he/she asks for something you cannot give right now but may be possible in the future, tell your inner child, be honest. This also may be a good opportunity to say I'm sorry to your inner child for any reason your inner child may have been hurt.

28. Promise your inner child now that you will always be there to protect and to nurture him/her.

29. It's time to leave. Ask him/her if you could come back to check in again in the future.

30. If your inner child agrees, give him/her the opportunity to say goodbye to these surroundings and promise that he/she can return whenever

he/she chooses. If your inner child wants to stay, give them the space and let them know that if he/she ever needs you, just call out and you will return. Let your inner child know it would be nice to be together again.

31. It's time to come back now. If desired, hug your inner child in gratitude for the time together.

32. Take a deep breath, stretch out all your muscles, begin to return to your surroundings, and open your eyes.

33. Journal your experience.

#7 Spiritual Mapping

SPIRITUAL LIFE MAPPING

A spiritual assessment

Spiritual life maps are a pictorial delineation of a person's spiritual journey. At its most basic level, a drawing pencil is used to sketch spiritually significant life events on paper. Thus, much like road maps, spiritual life maps tell us where we have come from, where we are now, and where we are going. The method is analogous to approaches drawn from art and family therapy in which a client's history is depicted on a "lifeline." However, the narrative is based on the person's spiritual pilgrimage and associated events. Put simply, a spiritual life map is an illustrated account of the person's timeline mapping his or her spiritual life. When gaining self-awareness of where you have been and what you have experienced, you can begin to have greater clarity of where you desire to go on your spiritual path. Spirituality is a journey! This assessment will help you appreciate the ride and be a co-creator of your destiny!

1. Get a poster board and begin drawing your life path. You can begin with knowledge as early as your mother's pregnancy with you (easy delivery, challenging, etc.) and other information attained by the family regarding your first 5 years. Then continue in 5-year increments.

2. As you post on your spiritual map, it is recommended that you journal your emotions when reflecting. "Do I remember how I felt at this time? How do I feel now as I'm thinking about it?"

3. As you reflect on your life path, it is common for other memories to begin emerging. Add them onto your mapping as you remember.

4. When completed, review your life and read your journal. This is your story! Use this exercise to better understand the importance of your life, how your personality has been sculpted, and how life gives us the opportunity to learn the necessary lessons in the challenges and joys we experience and helps us to realize our spiritual purpose.

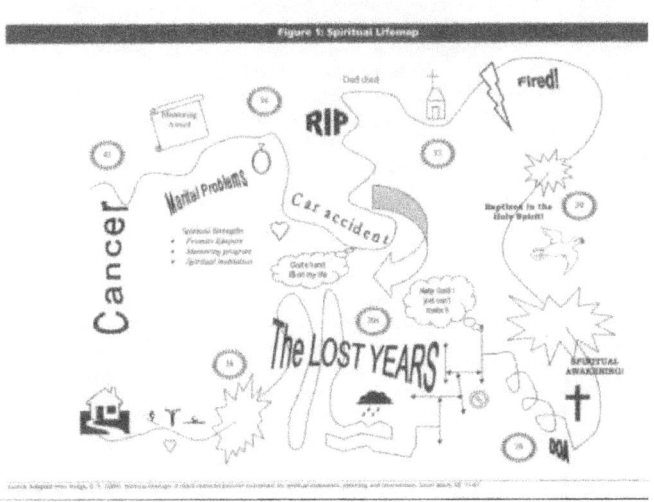

Figure 1: Spiritual Lifemap

#8 The Feeling Letter Technique

Purpose:

This is a letter that you would write when you are upset. It is done to expand your awareness, to incorporate positive, loving feelings without having to repress your negative emotions. *Dis-ease creates disease*. This exercise helps you to open your heart and let go of negative energy. No matter how much you may desire to have a good relationship, if your feelings are hurt… .it is difficult to be loving and supportive. This letter helps you give yourself the support you need when your partner/friend/parent/sibling, etc., can't!

What it is not:

This letter is not to dump resentment, judgment, and criticism on the other person. It is not written to try to change them or correct them, nor to point out their inadequacies. If it is used for this purpose, it will not work. The feeling letter works only when it is written for you to validate your feelings, let go and be able to open your heart again to be and feel more loving.

This is a skill that a person can learn to help them have a lasting, loving relationship. This technique helps a person learn how to release resentment and other negative feelings, to become centered in the positive attitudes of love, understanding, and forgiveness again.

First published in 1984 in the book, *What You Feel, You Can Heal* by John Gray, PhD, it has been rewritten

160

in three other best-selling books by other authors, and is used by numerous therapists, self-help groups, twelve-step programs, church groups, college counseling courses, and other support groups.

The Feeling Letter Technique is a method for processing and transforming negative feelings.

1. Anger

2. Sadness

3. Fear

4. Remorse

5. Love and other positive attitudes

As you write out your feelings at one level your awareness will naturally move to the feelings on the next level. Continue to write at each level until you have exhausted that feeling. As you write out the feelings at the first 3 levels, you may notice the emotions becoming more intense. This is a sign that you are letting go of these feelings, and a catharsis is taking place. It is important to go to level 5 and write out your positive feelings.

The Feeling Letter Technique has two parts:

1. Writing out the complete truth about how you feel, while imagining that you are being heard and understood.

2. Then writing a loving response to your letter. In this response letter, imagine the person to whom

you have written the letter responding with an open heart. Write a response expressing the feelings and acknowledgments that you need to hear.

*Please note that this is a process and takes time to complete. Open up your emotional valve and let your authentic feelings flow....

Part One: The Emotional Map

As you write out your feelings at one level, your awareness will naturally move to the feelings on the next level. Continue to write at each level until you have exhausted that feeling. As you write out the feelings at the first 3 levels, you may notice the emotions becoming more intense. This is a sign that you are letting go of these feelings, and a catharsis is taking place. It is important to go to level 5 and write out your positive feelings.

Please note that these are not one-word answers below. They are paragraphs of emotion. Follow the prompts and write until you exhaust all the emotion below each topic. There is no limit to what you may write for each statement.

Level 1:

<u>Anger</u>

I don't like.........

I resent.........

I feel frustrated.......

I feel angry.............

I feel furious..............

I want....................

Level 2:

Sadness

It hurts..........

I feel disappointed.........

I feel sad............

I feel unhappy...............

I wish............

Level 3:

Fear

It is painful.............

I feel worried..........

I feel afraid.............

I feel scared.............

I need......................

Level 4:

Remorse and Apologies

I apologize...........................

I feel embarrassed...............

I am sorry............................

I feel ashamed......................

I am willing...........................

Level 5:

<u>Love, Understanding,</u>

<u>Gratitude, & Forgiveness</u>

I love.......................

I appreciate.............

I realize.....................

I forgive....................

I would like.........

I trust..................

Part Two
The Response Letter

Take a few minutes to write a response to yourself. This can be the most healing part of this technique.

The response letter should include:

1. Apologies expressed in a way that make you feel heard and supported.

2. Understanding and validating statements

that expressed warmth and compassion for your feelings.

3. Loving statements that praise, appreciate, and acknowledge what you deserve.

4. Whatever else you need to hear to feel good.

By writing a response letter, your subconscious mind gets to feel and hear the support it deserves. Through being responsible to express what we need to hear, we open our hearts to feel and accept the support that does exist. When sharing it, you give this individual a chance to express love and support through the channel that will be most effective and fulfilling for you. It is through your own personal experience that you can be authentic to your emotions and begin to heal.

About the Authors

Dr. RoseMary Cairo: It is my true testament that life is full of miracles, but if we don't expect them, they are difficult to see. As a little girl of three years old, I lived a miracle that would change the course of my life. I didn't ask for it, but many people prayed for this miracle because they knew that there was a force far greater than our imagination, science and reality, a divine power that could save the world, one miracle at a time. They believed...

I was born into an Italian/Sicilian family; my father was born in Calabria, Italy and my mother's grandparents were born in Palermo, Sicily. Faith was never questioned nor was the truth of Jesus being our Savior. Prayers, novenas and the rosary were the 911 channel to the Lord and my father's family had at least one religious relic on them at all times.

The day I got sick, my family and I were visiting my maternal grandparents, who lived in a two-flat in Chicago. I had a sore throat and before the end of the night, I had a fever and began to cough deep and often. Within a short amount of time, I had trouble breathing and had a high fever of 105. My parents and I were soon swept into a police car owned by the police officer that lived above my grandparent's flat. He insisted upon driving us to St. Anne's Hospital in Chicago, as he observed my breathing becoming more challenged.

My cough and labored breathing were given a diagnosis of 'Croup', and before the doctors could treat me, my trachea (windpipe) closed, and they performed an emergency tracheotomy in the hallway of St. Anne's hospital. For one month, I stayed in the hospital, in an oxygen tent, getting multiple shots per day to help me fight croup and prevent secondary infections, with the greatest enemy being... pneumonia. The doctors warned my parents that if I contracted pneumonia, only a miracle would save me. They had no antibiotics that were strong enough to combat pneumonia in my poor state of health. Laying in an oxygen tent for one month, receiving multiple shots per day in a 3-year-old body and struggling to recover, I caught staff pneumonia in both lungs. The doctors came to my parents and painfully told them that they did not have a remedy to cure the pneumonia. One of the doctors leaned over to my mother and said, "You need to pray for a miracle because only God can save her."

After my parents cried in disbelief and realized how terminal this was, they knew they would have to give this cross up to God. All our family, friends and their circles of extended family and friends began a prayer chain, lighting candles and saying novenas and rosaries. That night, Jesus came to me. I can envision this moment as if it was yesterday. Across from the metal-spindled crib that I laid in was a crucifix on the wall and to the right of me, behind where my mom sat, was a window. Burning with fever, I held my mother's pinkie finger through the spindles. I can remember looking at the wall in front of me where the crucifix was, but instead of Jesus on the cross, He appeared life-size in front of me. He seemed suspended in the air, and He smiled at me. He stretched his arms out to me and brought them into his chest repeatedly with a beautiful expression of peace in his eyes.

I can still feel this immeasurable abundance of love as it seeped through my small, sick body and filled my heart. In the window, just to the right of the crib, was an angel surrounded by bright light. I took my finger and pointed to Jesus, trying to tell my mom that Jesus was in the room and my angel was going to help take me to heaven with him, but because of the tracheotomy, I couldn't talk. She was reading my lips, screaming as she began to understand what I was saying. No one could see the visions but me, yet my parents' faith told them that my spirit was going to go to Jesus, and I was going to die. My father fell to his knees, begging God to spare me and my mother ran for the doctors in hopes that they could save me and prevent me from what seemed to be my destiny. All I can remember is Jesus smiling at me, permeating me with love and my angel that illuminated the room. My next memory is waking up in the morning with my parents and doctors around me. It was at some point, between my vision of Christ and my guardian angel and waking up the next morning, that I was completely cured of Staff pneumonia in both of my lungs. Many doctors came to see me that day. They told my parents never to ask God for a miracle because I am their miracle and the miracle of St. Anne's Hospital. A few days later, I was a happy, healthy, three-year-old little girl and I was able to go home.

This is my testimony, not a repeated story of someone else's experience. A time in the life of a 3-year-old little girl who was graced with a miracle that created a significant shift in the lives of those who were at the hospital that day and those who heard and continue to hear of this heavenly intersession of love, prayer, and faith. Could this be the imagination of a little girl fighting for her life or the truth of the Lord and His messenger, who came to create a divine intervention for a child that would grow up to share her story of a miracle granted by the Lord Jesus Christ? This moment in time put me on a spiritual path that taught me that divine intercession can come when we are the most vulnerable, communicated by prayer, and delivered by God and His angels. It created a profound relationship between me and Jesus, my Savior. Miracles happen every day! We choose what we want to believe, but miracles aren't our choice… just believing in them is. Pay attention because no matter what you believe, they are happening all around us…

In Light & Love – RoseMary

Alberto Minzer: Since the writing of my first book, *BOYS DON'T CRY: MEN DO*, published in 2006, much has happened in my life. The book was written in my thirties. I was married with two children. It has been fifteen years.

Since this writing, many changes have occurred in my life. I am remarried and I have three grandchildren. Looking back, I see a different man. The man I was in 2006 is not the same man today. I am more at ease with myself. I am more comfortable in my own skin. I have an acceptance of myself and others. I am actually free from the messages I grew up with and no longer driven to succeed through materialistic means. I know the difference between need and desire. I am much wiser and connected to myself and others. I am more trusting of myself and more intuitive of what the Creator's will is versus my own.

The birth of my grandchildren brought me to a new phase in my life where I stepped into a deeper gratitude and awe of life's miracles and blessings. The birth of my second grandson literally brought me to my knees and made me aware of a deeper lack I had and did not know until his circumcision. This is quite intense for me since I had the honor to hold him while he was being circumcised in an orthodox Jewish congregation. During his circumcision, I was surrounded by at least 100 orthodox men or so singing and coming towards me in the pulpit. As I held my grandson, their loving energy was so intense that I was pierced energetically by their love and joy, and it hit me right then and there in the deepest parts of myself where I lacked self-love. I could not fully receive the love that was coming my way.

I began a deeper introspective search and began a more intense self-study of my relationship with the creator. I began to study Kabbala and became a Sufi student. This took me back to deeper layers of all the issues I thought I dealt with but were still there in my heart. I began to purify all those places that needed to be cleaned, let go and released. Despite the many years in therapy and self-examination, these powerful spiritual studies showed me there were still traces of deeper layers of self-shame, grief, lack of love and self-acceptance.

I learned to connect with the light of God and to my astonishment, I began to be filled up and no longer felt a lack, an emptiness inside me. The connection to God's light has deepened my understanding that at the deepest levels of self, all the light of God is revealed. By living in this light, I can serve myself and others in a good way. I lack nothing and give without needing anything back. Unconditional love is not just a word. It's an experience.

In Service – Alberto